The Secret Garden

The Secret Garden of the Soul

An Introduction to the Kabbalah

ALLAN ARMSTRONG

FOREWORD BY R. A. GILBERT

IMAGIER PUBLISHING
BRISTOL, 2008

First published in 2008 by
Imagier Publishing
Rookery Farm
Bristol, BS35 3SY
United Kingdom
E-mail: ip@imagier.com
www.imagier.com

ISBN 10: 0-955815-0-X
ISBN 13: 978-0-955815-0-7

Cover and text design by Valerie Cooper
Cover image is adapted from 'The Tree of the Soul' by D. A.
Freher, in *Works of Jacob Behmen*, Law edition, 1764.
The paper used in this publication is from a sustainable
source and is elemental chlorine free.

Printed and bound by CPI Antony Rowe, Eastbourne
18 17 16 15 14 13 12 11 10 09 08
10 9 8 7 6 5 4 3 2 1

Contents

Illustrations

Acknowledgements

THIS BOOK BEGAN its life in the mid-1980's as a collection of 'Notes on Kabbalah' intended for those students just beginning their studies of the subject. It has evolved through the many discussions that took place around it, and I will ever be grateful to the many students who each in their own unique way precipitated the development of this book.

I owe a debt of gratitude to Val Cooper for her patience in editing and setting this book. Her support and patient hard work has been a source of encouragement from the start. Also to the author, scholar, and leading authority on the Western Hermetic tradition, R. A. Gilbert, who patiently read through several versions of the manuscript, correcting errors and offering constructive advice concerning the coherence and clarity of the text. But most of all to my wife 'Glo', whose unfailing support and tolerance over the course of many years allowed this book to happen.

Foreword

W E DO NOT come easily to the experience of spiritual reality—the very concept is ill-defined and its very existence as a reality is denied by the materialists who are the current arbiters of what should and should not constitute the 'real' in the thought and experience of Western culture. And yet, for those who do have faith in God, there is an internal drive that fuels our constant desire to seek and to find a path that will lead us to such experience: the vision of what is spiritually real, and the further way by which we may come to know that reality in our ultimate union with God. Kabbalah, as this book shows, is just such a path.

Of course, it is neither an easy nor a certain way. Its symbols are strange and often ambiguous, its structure is complex, and systematic analysis of its content is a long, difficult, and problematic process. And the symbolic map of that content—the glittering image of the Tree of Life—can glamorise the unwary, just as it can also set the wise pilgrim on a true path to spiritual fulfilment.

The first problem encountered on any path that leads to spiritual experience, and to an understanding of the meaning that such an experience has for us, is that of formulating a language in which we can speak about it. Because the quest for spiritual reality, the processes involved in attaining an experience of such a reality, and the words with which we can communicate the experience—to our own memory as well as to others—all fall outside the normal range of everyday discourse, we must find or develop a new and appropriate vocabulary. Until we can do this we can neither comprehend spiritual experience, nor communicate our understanding of it. Without this new language we cannot justify the reality of non-empirical experience, even to ourselves.

The Language of Mysticism

Traditionally the descriptive language of spiritual experience, especially that exalted form of it that is true mystical experience, is paradoxical: the direct experience of God is described indirectly, by using simile, metaphor, analogy, and symbol. The words and imagery will vary from age to age and from faith to faith, but there are clear parallels between the reports of all mystics. Thus the Christian may capture his or her exaltation by relating it to verbal or pictorial symbols of the presence of Christ, while the Jewish mystic may seek to express the experience in terms of combining the letters of the Ineffable Name. Both, however, will insist that no words, ordinarily used, can adequately convey the nature and meaning of the experience.

The 16th-century Spanish mystic, St. Teresa of Avila, lamented the impossibility of doing verbal justice to her experience of ecstatic visionary states. She sets her detailed, flowing reports of them in the context of the human image of Christ, but recognises the limitations of her attempts to describe them:

I wish I could give a description of at least the smallest part of what I learned, but, when I try to discover
a way of doing so, I find it impossible; for, while the
light we see here and that other light are both light,
there is no comparison between the two ... In short,
however skilful the imagination may be, it will not
succeed in picturing or describing what that light is
like, nor a single one of those things which I learned
from the Lord with a joy so sovereign as to be inde-
scribable. . . . I cannot possibly explain how this hap-
pened, but without seeing anything, I seemed to see
myself in the presence of the Godhead.[1]

Other mystics who entered similar exalted states, found
that even basic description failed. Is it even correct to speak
of 'entering' a state utterly apart from the material? Writing
about his own experience, A. E. Waite acknowledged that,

... in attempting to convey an impression I am under
the penalty of words which fail everywhere and communicate nothing but antithesis. The state is not entered
and one does not come out therefrom: we are simply in
it and subsequently we are not in it, but amidst a terrible experience of lost beatitude in reality.[2]

And yet mystics have always written and spoken about
their experiences; it is part of the price to be paid for succeeding in the spiritual quest, and for receiving God in the
heart. Waite wrote of this also, using the language of a Christian Kabbalist:

And those who enter into this state come back into
the world, with the yoke of the kingdom upon them
in a law of service. Then God shall give them work. Of
such it is said in the Zohar that the world is sustained
by the voice of little children reading the Law.[3]

---

[1] Saint Teresa of Jesus, *The Complete Works, Vol. 1: The Life*, E. Allison Peers,
trans. and ed. (London: Sheed & Ward, 1946) pp. 268, 273.
[2] A. E. Waite, *Lamps of Western Mysticism: Essays on the Life of the Soul in
God* (London: Kegan Paul, 1923), pp. 325–326.
[3] *Ibid.*, p. 330.

This has a resonance with the ideas of some Jewish mystics, who accepted that the ability to communicate the essence of mystical experience may be God-given. Thus the medieval mystic Abraham Abulafia wrote of Kabbalists who sought the secrets of the Divine Name that,

> ... they ascend from light to light ... to the union, until their inner speech returns, cleaving to the primordial speech which is the source of all speech, and they further ascend from speech to speech until the inner human speech [is a] power in itself, and he prepares himself to receive the Divine speech, whether in the aspect of the image of speech, whether in the aspect of the speech itself; and these are the prophets in truth, in justice and righteousness.[4]

All of this emphasises the importance of an adequate descriptive language for mystical experience: it is not simply to enable the mystic to give an account of his or her spiritual adventures, but to ensure that the life-enhancing essence of the experience can be communicated to others for their spiritual benefit. But here another problem arises. The mystic must first speak to the people of his own time and place, framing his experience in words and images that they will understand. Then comes the further task of translating accurately what the mystic relates into the languages of other ages and other faiths. At every stage the blinding light of the original vision dims a little more. How, then, can the light be preserved?

The initial vision, exaltation, revelation, or illumination— and there are many other words appropriate to the 'otherness' of spiritual experience—may come from a divine source, but the mystic, and his or her hearers, are human, with all the limitations of human beings. We do not understand the physiology of the interface between the material and the

---

[4] Abulafia, *We-zot li-Yehudah*. Quoted in Moshe Idel, *The Mystical Experience in Abraham Abulafia* (Albany: SUNY Press, 1988), p. 83.

spiritual—between the empirical and the non-empirical, the rational and the non-rational, the ephemeral and the eternal —but it is the means by which the experience of the mystic is preserved in his memory, translated into rational thought and speech and given out as spoken or written words to the world at large. In its passage into and through the mystic, the message, the sum of his experience and its meaning, may become diluted or distorted, which is why the construction of a coherent and consistent language of mystical experience, a language that is both synthetic and analytic, is so important. It cannot rely solely on words, however they may be arranged into metaphorical, parabolic, or symbolic form, but must include visual and auditory components: combinations of shapes, colours, and sounds that will form meaningful images for those who see and hear them.

How this is done, the precise method by which the mystic's experience of other realms or states of being is encapsulated in words and images, will vary according to the society, era, and faith in which he or she lives. But there will be undoubted parallels that cross cultural and religious boundaries, for the source of the true mystical experience must always be the same, by whatever name we may know it. The visual imagery of widely different cultures and faiths will have common elements, as will their poetry and their vocal and instrumental music. All of these are called upon by the mystic when building the language of spiritual experience.

And when the language is complete it must do more than simply record the inner and outer events of the mystic's life: it must convey to us the manner of following in the footsteps of the mystic, and the purpose in our doing so. Ideally such a language will cross human boundaries of faith and society, and will become a timeless, universal support for all those who seek the path to a direct experience of God. It will not be constructed easily and there are some boundaries that are supremely difficult to cross: there is, for example, no rational path linking faith in a personal God with pantheistic beliefs. But this problem does not arise for the three great religions of the West, grounded as they are in a common conception of God as both creator and saviour, whose will has been divinely revealed.

There are, of course, great differences in the manner in which Christian, Jewish, and Muslim mystics have presented their visions, revelations, and exaltations, but there is a common foundation beneath the surface divisions, and a systematic approach to codifying the relationship between God and humanity, the nature and unfolding of creation, and the processes at work in spiritual experience, is both possible and desirable. To a very significant degree the Kabbalah, which has successfully transcended the limitations of its original cultural environment, and which possesses a comprehensive symbolic language, provides such an approach.

The Tree of Life

The Kabbalah is not, however, simply a universal schematic presentation of the Way to God—it is rooted in the Torah, the divine law that lies at the heart of the Jewish faith, and encompasses also a rich treasury of literary texts: commentaries on the Torah, and analyses of its hidden meanings; narratives of the lives and work of Kabbalists down the ages; pious legends; and practical instruction on prayer and meditation. But the Kabbalah is not confined to Judaism: it is a path to the direct experience of the divine that is open to other believers in the one God, and for the active Western seeker after Him, the most significant aspect of the Kabbalah will be the symbolic, while the principal symbol that he or she will encounter is the Tree of Life. This powerful image appears at the beginning of the Old Testament, in the first book of the Torah, and at the end of the New—in the closing chapter of the Revelation that completes the Christian scriptures. No other symbol could be more appropriate for both Jewish and Christian Kabbalists.

But what precisely is a symbol? A symbol, usually a material object or its image, represents or denotes something else that is immaterial or abstract, such as a moral or intellectual trait, an idea, a spiritual truth, or a spiritual presence. In the context of religious experience there must be an acceptance of the faith to which the symbol applies, and of the truth of what it presents in symbolic form for it to have meaning for those who see and make use of it. Thus the symbols present in religious worship give meaning to the public expression of the quest for divine union, just as they, and analogous symbols, also provide a focus for private prayer and contemplation.

Symbols may be simple pictorial images, or vast and complex constructions, such as Gothic cathedrals, which symbolise the Trinity in their tripartite division of choir, or nave, and aisles, and represent redemption in their cross-shaped form. Just such a combination of numerical and conceptual symbolism is also central to the Kabbalistic Tree of Life, which presents the journey to the presence of God by way of a symbolic path from root to crown through the ten subtly interlinked Sephiroth. There is, of course, much more to it than this; the symbols displayed in depictions of the Tree, whether plain diagrams, decorative engravings, or paintings, tend to be deceptively simple. They can simultaneously reveal to the devout seeker hidden elements of the relationship between creation and the creator, and conceal what is sacred from the defiling curiosity of the materialist.

The Sephirotic Tree of Life is also a ubiquitous image, presented all too often, and with little or no justification, as a unifying emblem of the many disparate parts of the Western Hermetic Tradition. Such a view of the central structural feature of the Kabbalah is both inadequate and inaccurate, but it is an inevitable consequence of the modern desire for easy enlightenment, for instant understanding of the complexities of the spiritual life.

For those who would embrace the Western Hermetic Tradition as the embodiment of the theory and practise of the way of divine union, and who would explore the rich storehouse of its spiritual treasures, it is essential first to see what the Tree of Life really is, to see it as a living entity, and not simply to look at it as an historical relic in a museum of symbolic images. In order to do this, one must enter the Secret Garden of the Soul, contemplate what is there and strive to understand it. And this, of course, requires a guide that will safely direct the seeker on both the theoretical and practical paths, while setting the Tree of Life in its historical and philosophical contexts, and systematically explaining its structure and nature. This book, whose title explains its purpose, provides that guide, although it makes no pretence of being a comprehensive handbook to Kabbalistic philosophy and practise.

It is, indeed, impossible to gain a full understanding of the Kabbalah in all its aspects from any one text, however inspired it may be, even were it possible—which it is not—for any individual to do so in the course of an earthly lifetime. But the ability to set out on the path toward such a goal, which is also the Way of Divine Union, does lie within the grasp of each of us, and we shall go the more easily and the more readily along that path with the aid of this compact introduction by an experienced Kabbalist who is also a skilled spiritual director.

Allan Armstrong presents the Kabbalah in a manner that engages the reader. He defines the terms of its specialised language, unfolds the origins and history of the Judeo-Christian mystical tradition that is encapsulated in the Kabbalah, and records the lives and work of the illuminated visionaries and mystics who developed a coherent form in which to present it systematically. But what distinguishes this book is the way in which the novice is guided through the pitfalls in what is commonly known in Western esoteric circles as 'Practical Kabbalah'. This is, perhaps, an unfortunate term, because it is used as a container for both the traditional methods of prayer and meditation employed by Kabbalists from the early medieval period down to the present day, and the more unsafe, and often morally dubious, processes of Western occultism.

These 'occult' processes tend to concentrate on techniques of visualization, often of angelic forms, based partly upon the perceived significance of the complex numerical and lexical analyses of biblical texts developed by Kabbalists in the past, and partly upon the psycho-spiritual effect of particular ways of uttering divine names. Such processes are not to be lightly taken up, even by those who have been deeply immersed in the Kabbalah for the whole of their adult lives, and they are definitely not for the novice. Mr. Armstrong is wise in pointing out that the Kabbalah is not a path for those 'with a casual interest or dilettante attitude' toward it, nor, it must be emphasised, is there the slightest merit to be gained in following what might best be termed the 'commercial Kabbalah'. All self-styled Kabbalists who expect or demand a financial reward for teaching the doctrines and practises of this God-given tradition are nothing but blasphemers who prostitute their talents for worldly gain. They have nothing and they can give nothing.

But for those who eschew occultist distortions of Kabbalistic texts, and whose goal in life is spiritual regeneration and ultimate reintegration with the divine, a genuine commitment to prayer and meditation centred on the central

images of the Kabbalah will prove to be a spiritually reward-
ing path. And it is not a restricted or sectarian path. For the
Jewish Kabbalist, the Tree of Life can be perceived as a path
that leads at once down from the creator to His creation and
up from the human to the divine, just as the angels passed up
and down the ladder in Jacob's dream. A parallel image for
the Christian Kabbalistic mystic is that of Thomas Traherne,
who saw the Cross of Christ as the Jacob's Ladder by which
we ascend to God. Kabbalistic texts and imagery stand above
the divisions of human religions and do not require us to
deny our own faith.

They are not, however, instantly accessible to the seeker:
enthusiasm, piety, and intelligence are not enough. We still
need our guide through the labyrinth of the Kabbalah, and
The Secret Garden of the Soul is admirably equipped to send us
on our way. It neither can, nor does it pretend to take us up
to a direct experience of God, but it sets out all those aspects
of the Kabbalah that we can and should seek to study and to
understand; and it provides us with a glossary of the strange
terms that we will encounter, biographical notes on both
Jewish and Christian Kabbalists of the past; and an admirably well-chosen bibliography for further study.

Above all the entire text is built around presenting the
Kabbalah as it truly is: the essential Western path for the
interior journey of the human spirit back to God.

R. A. Gilbert,
Tickenham, North Somerset,
December 2007

Chapter 1

The Development of
the Tradition

IN THE EYES of scholars, Kabbalah is generally perceived as
an esoteric system of spiritual development that emerged
within medieval Judaism. However, many respected Kabbalists
believe that Kabbalah is far older than this; that it is nothing
less than the secret doctrine of spiritual development, transmitted to the people of Israel through the prophet Moses
more than three millennia ago. But from either viewpoint
the impact of Kabbalah upon the deep waters of mysticism
and magic has been both extensive and significant. Indeed,
ever since the Kabbalah first emerged from the shadows of
the sanctuary, in the late twelfth century, its teachings have
not only influenced the mystical and spiritual life of Judaism,
but have also contributed to the shape and spiritual direc-
tion of some of the Western world's foremost metaphysical
institutions and esoteric movements—Rosicrucianism and
Freemasonry among them—and have been central to such
movements from the Renaissance to the present day.

Given such a pedigree it is intriguing that less than fifty
years ago there were few books available in the English language about this influential albeit obscure system of spiritual development. Indeed, before the turn of the twentieth

century there were scarcely any. One, titled *The Kabbalah: Its Doctrines, Development and Literature*, written by Dr. C. D. Ginsburg, had been published in 1865, but was not easily obtained until it was republished in the twentieth century. It was the first objective work on the subject to be published in English since the seventeenth century and has been very influential in esoteric circles; indeed, it still commands a great deal of respect. Another, *The Kabbalah Unveiled*, translated by S.L.M. Mathers from the Latin of Knorr von Rosenroth, was published in 1887. It contains three Kabbalistic texts from the Zohar: The Lesser Holy Assembly; The Greater Holy Assembly; and The Book of Concealed Mystery. Today this book is criticised by many orthodox Jewish Kabbalists; nevertheless, it must be acknowledged that ever since its first publication it has been extremely influential among Western esotericists, and Mathers's introduction is still thought to be a valuable contribution to the subject. These two books, together with *Qabbalah, the Philosophical Writings of Solomon Ben Yehudah Ibn Gebirol*, published in 1888 by American scholar Isaac Myer, were, in the late nineteenth century, the most readily available works in the English language concerning Kabbalah.

During the twentieth century this situation changed as more books concerning this little-known subject became available. Many, but by no means all, were written by members of a well-known, yet short-lived, esoteric Christian Rosicrucian order known as the Hermetic Order of the Golden Dawn. Kabbalah was fundamental to its workings, and W. Wynn Westcott, one of the founder members of this order, wrote a simple yet interesting introduction titled *The Kabbalah*, which was published in 1910. Arthur Edward Waite, another member, wrote a deeper study of the secret doctrine of Israel titled *The Doctrine and Literature of the Kabalah*, which was published in 1902, and republished with considerably more information in 1929. Other authors with connections to the Hermetic Order of the Golden Dawn, and who published books about the Kabbalah, were Henry Pullen-Bury, Dion Fortune, and Israel Regardie. Dion Fortune's book, *The Mystical Qabalah* (published in 1935), is a basic interpretation of the Tree of Life from a magical perspective; it is still in demand in some circles. Israel Regardie's book *The Garden of Pomegranates*, first published in 1932 is also a study of the Tree of Life and follows a line of enquiry broadly similar to Dion Fortune's book.

During the last fifty years or so a great many more books have been written in the English language about the Kabbalah. One of the most notable aspects of this outpouring of material has been the contribution made by members of the Jewish community, who have made a significant amount of valuable Kabbalistic material accessible to the English-speaking world. Yet, although this proliferation has vastly increased the information available, it is still true to say that the nature of the Kabbalah not only remains obscure and consequently the subject of a great deal of speculative uncertainty, but its history is still concealed in the mists of antiquity—which is, perhaps, as it should be.

One of the most outstanding Jewish scholars of the twentieth century, the late Gershom Scholem, stated that: 'The Kabbalah, is literally 'Tradition,' that is, the tradition of things divine, it is the sum of Jewish mysticism'.[1] The word 'Kabbalah' itself is derived from the Hebrew, QBL—Qibel—a word that means 'to receive', and there are many different ways of spelling the word Kabbalah in English; the most common being *Kabbalah*, *Qabalah*, and *Cabala*. However, it should be noted that such variations are common with Hebrew and Arabic words that are translated into English, as there are several different systems of transliterating Hebrew and Arabic alphabets into Roman letters. Furthermore, the spelling

---

[1] Gershom Scholem, *On the Kabbalah and Its Symbolism* (New York: Schocken, 1996), p 1.

of the word with one or two b's is equally appropriate insofar as the single 'b' accurately reflects the Hebrew spelling of the word, while the double 'b' more accurately describes the pronunciation. Therefore, one should not be unduly concerned about the correct spelling of the word in English.

The word 'Kabbalah' signifies a body of knowledge passed on by oral transmission and is closely related in meaning to what we understand in English by the word 'tradition'. There are many traditions within Judaism, but in reality there is only one that is concerned with the oral transmission of the essential esoteric teachings of Jewish mysticism; it is a subject concerned, as is all true mysticism, not only with our union with the divine but also with the nature, source, destiny, and chemistry of consciousness, and as such has been central to the development of Western esoteric thought from the earliest times. This development can be thought of as having taken place in ten stages.

THE FIRST STAGE: THE REVELATION OF THE NEW DISPENSATION

It is generally accepted that the Kabbalah emerged in southern Europe during the closing years of the twelfth century, particularly in the region of southern France and eastern Spain. The defining moments of this era are marked by the emergence of two literary creations: the *Sefer ha Bahir* (The Book of Brilliance, commonly referred to as the Bahir) and the *Sefer ha Zohar* (The Book of Splendour, also referred to as the Zohar). Appearing in Provence in the latter half of the twelfth century, the Bahir explores, among other things, the Tree of Life and the thirty-two paths of wisdom. The Zohar—composed, it is believed, by Moses de Leon between 1280 and 1286—is a mystical commentary on the Pentateuch, the first five books of

---

2   Gershom Scholem, *Kabbalah* (Jerusalem: Keter Publishing, 1974), p. 57.

the Bible.[2] It is probably the case that these texts in one form or another were in private circulation at an earlier date, but as yet there is no solid evidence to support this supposition. In some respects, placing the origins of Kabbalah in medieval Europe is somewhat misleading as the essential ideas in Kabbalah had for many centuries previously played an important role in the life of Jewish mysticism, and that Kabbalists of all eras have maintained that it was Moses himself who transmitted the essence of the Kabbalah to the people of ancient Israel. From this point of view, Kabbalah was not a medieval invention but evolved over time, beginning with Moses.

Who, then, was Moses? Biblical historians believe he flourished during the thirteenth century B.C. His life is described in Exodus, the second book of the Old Testament, where we are informed that he was born of Jewish parents and through curious circumstances was adopted by and brought up as a member of the Egyptian royal family. We are further informed that he was instructed in all of the ancient wisdom of Egypt, and was also instructed in the wisdom of the surrounding nations.[3] Eventually, with divine assistance, he emancipated the Jewish people from the yoke of Egyptian oppression and led them out of the land of Egypt into the wilderness, where he formed them into a nation, finally leading them to the 'Promised Land'.

Important as these achievements undoubtedly were, from the point of view of this work there was another event of far greater significance. In the third month of the people of Israel's sojourn in the wilderness, Moses ascended Mount Sinai, where he received a dispensation from God for the Jewish people.[4] This new dispensation was at first transmitted to the people of Israel by Moses alone, but following

---

[3] Acts 7, 22; See also *Josephus Complete Works*, W. Whiston, trans. (Grand Rapids, Michigan: Kregel, 1978), Book II ch. 9, sect. 6, p. 57, and *The Works of Philo*, C. D. Yonge, trans. (Peabody, MA: Hendrickson, 1995), p. 461.

[4] Exodus 19 in The New King James Version of the Bible (Nashville: Thomas Nelson, 1982). All subsequent biblical references, unless otherwise stated, are to this version.

divine instruction he gathered seventy elders together, and the Lord 'took the spirit that was upon Moses and put it upon the seventy elders'.[5] Through this transmission the elders not only received a spiritual insight into the meaning of the Mosaic Law that had been established for the social well-being of the people, but also an understanding of the soul of the Law (*Torah*) that had been established for the spirit of the people. In this lies the source of the Jewish tradition we know as Kabbalah.

The Second Stage: From the Seventy Elders to the Babylonian Invasion

The essential teachings embodied in the Torah, both in its exoteric and esoteric form, were transmitted orally from generation to generation until the early part of the sixth century B.C., when Israel was invaded by the Babylonian army under the leadership of their king, Nebuchadnezzar (605–562 B.C.). The royal family and the ruling elite were taken into captivity with many of the more skilled artisans and craftsmen. Thus began the Babylonian Exile (597 B.C.), from which year the prophet Ezekiel, who was among the captives, dates his calculations. In 586 B.C., Zedekiah, the new king of Judea, after taking an oath of fealty to Nebuchadnezzar, planned an insurrection against him.[6] Nebuchadnezzar responded by sending an army against Jerusalem. The siege lasted for a year and a half, at the end of which Nebuchadnezzar ordered the Temple, he royal palace, and all dwellings in the city to be destroyed by fire, and the surviving inhabitants to be taken captive into Babylon. The Babylonians sacked Jerusalem, destroyed the Temple, and carried off many thousands of people to serve as slaves in Babylon. However, many evaded captivity by fleeing into other lands and living in exile. Thus began the Diaspora,

---

[5] Septuagint (London: Bagster, 1879), Numbers XI 24–25.

[6] Ezek. 17:13.

which was to have a profound influence upon the future of Judaism.[7]

<h2 align="center">THE THIRD STAGE: COMMITTING THE
ORAL TRADITION TO WRITING</h2>

During their captivity in Babylon, which lasted for seventy years, the essence of the Mosaic teachings (the Torah), which had been transmitted orally by Moses and the seventy elders, was committed to writing and gathered together in one work.[8] This work is the written Torah, and consists of the first five books of the Bible: Genesis, Exodus, Leviticus, Numbers, and Deuteronomy.

After the death of Nebuchadnezzar in 562 B.C., Babylon, weakened by internal dissensions, fell to the expanding empire of the Persians. During the reign of King Cyrus the Persian rule was benign, especially compared with the policies of the Assyrians and Babylonians, and the people of Babylon welcomed Cyrus as a liberator. He responded by treating the people generously, forbidding his troops from persecuting the people, allowing them to worship their gods unhindered. Cyrus's policy of tolerance and acceptance of cultural and religious diversity characterised his reign. In 538 B.C., Cyrus allowed the people of Judea to return home and ordered the rebuilding of the Jerusalem Temple. He returned the vessels that had been looted from the Temple, and even committed funds from his treasury to aid the project.[9]

---

[7] Diaspora: A term for Jewish communities living in foreign lands that resulted from the dispersion of the Jewish people at the time of the Babylonian invasion in 597 B.C.

[8] *Encyclopedia Judaica*, vol. 4 (Jerusalem: Keter, 1971), p. 823. 'It may safely be assumed that the work of final collection, fixing, and preservation of the Torah took place in the Babylonian Exile (*cf.* Ezra 7:14, 25). If some formal ceremony or act of canonization occurred, tradition has preserved no recollection of this momentous event'.

[9] Ezra 1:2–11, 6:3–5.

Upon returning from Babylon the Jewish people rebuilt the Temple and integrated the synagogue[10] (which had been instituted during their captivity as an alternative place of worship to the destroyed temple) into their religious life, with the reading and exposition of the Torah as its main objective. This was a very important development because it is the exposition of the esoteric interpretation of the Torah and of its language that constitutes the basis of the Tradition we call Kabbalah. And it was in the culture and spirit of the synagogue that it acquired its principal form and nature.

Although the people of Israel were no longer in exile, Israel remained a subject state dependent upon a succession of contemporary superpowers, eventually becoming a province of the Roman Empire. Under the rule of the various administrations put in place by Rome, Israel became a hotbed of internal conflict and insurrection. Jewish factions not only fought each other but also fought the Roman administration, making the government of the region impossible. Eventually, in A.D. 66, the Jews revolted against the Romans and a bloody war began. In response, Rome dispatched an army to restore order and a bloody war ensued.

By the year A.D. 68, resistance in the country had been eliminated and the Romans turned their full attention upon Jerusalem. The Roman legions, led by Titus, surrounded and laid siege to the city. In A.D. 70, they breached the outer walls and began a systematic demolition of the city. The assault culminated in the burning and destruction of the Temple. With this second destruction of the Temple, and the general demolition of the city itself, the war effectively came to an end. The Romans, making an example of the city, slaughtered many thousands of the inhabitants; any spared from death were taken as slaves or sent to the arena. Those who were able fled, seeking refuge in the many settlements of the Diaspora. Thus, from that time the Jews were 'a dis-

---

[10]   *Encyclopedia Judaica*, vol.15, p. 580.

persed people'; a nation without a state, and a religion without a temple. However, in the Diaspora Jewish refugees were able to establish a community, and preserved their identity in their religion.

THE FOURTH STAGE: THE GREEK INFLUENCE UPON THE DIASPORA

The Jews of the Diaspora were necessarily compelled to adapt to the more diverse cultural influences of the Greco-Roman world, whose major centres of civilisation had become a fusion of many different cultures. This they did, and in spite of all obstacles they successfully established communities throughout the Mediterranean world. Indeed, ancient writers, such as Josephus and Tacitus, record that the Diaspora Jews were both numerous (Jews constituted ten percent or more of the population of the Roman Empire)[11] and wealthy. This process had been greatly facilitated by Alexander the Great in the fourth century B.C., when he and his army opened up the world that lay beyond Mediterranean civilisation. The dispersed communities of Judaism—the Diaspora—took full advantage of the opportunities Alexander had made available and over the course of time established thriving communities in almost every city of the Roman Empire.

Around 331 B.C., Alexander the Great founded the celebrated city of Alexandria on the northern coast of Egypt, wherein mystery schools and religions of many different cultures established themselves, exchanging ideas and teachings, competing, comparing, and exploring new avenues of thought. It was in this vibrant city that the Jews, invited by Alexander himself, were to form a community of considerable size and strength. They contributed greatly to the life and reputation of Alexandria, which was to become a melt-

---

11 Feldman and Reinhold, *Jewish Life and Thought among the Greeks and Romans* (Edinburgh: T & T Clark, Ltd., 1996), p. 266.

ing pot of ideas and a centre of knowledge and wisdom that rivalled Athens and Eleusis. In the early part of the third century B.C., the first five books[12] of the Hebrew Bible were translated into the Greek language by seventy-two Jewish scholars. This translation subsequently became known as the *Septuagint*, the word meaning 'seventy' in Greek. According to the apocryphal letter of Aristeas,[13] six elders from each of the twelve tribes of Israel were invited to Alexandria by Ptolemy II to translate the scriptures—the five Mosaic books—into Greek. Over the course of the following two centuries the Septuagint eventually encompassed the rest of the Old Testament and other noncanonical books.

The Jews of the Diaspora had a reputation for being zealous missionaries, who sought, and often succeeded, in converting gentiles to the faith of the Torah. However, the influence went both ways; Greek thought also influenced and modified the religious practises of the Diaspora. Indeed, many Diaspora synagogues, particularly in Alexandria, held their services in the Greek language, much to the dismay of orthodox Jews in Israel. Furthermore, much of the Wisdom teaching was inspired by the Greeks and had a profound affect upon the esoteric understanding of the Torah. It is worth noting that after the great dispersion the Jews were for a considerable time without a spiritual or political centre. The rabbinical influence was slow to spread and the Talmud[14] evolved slowly—over some four hundred years or more. Inevitably, then, the beliefs of the people of the Diaspora were influenced by the cultural environment they found themselves in. Such environments, especially from the time of Alexander the Great, were more often than

[12] The five Mosaic books: Genesis, Exodus, Leviticus, Numbers, and Deuteronomy.

[13] R. H. Charles, *Apocrypha and Pseudepigrapha of the Old Testament*, vol. II (Oxford: Clarendon Press, 1913), pp. 82–122.

[14] Talmud: A collection of commentaries on the nature, regulation, and administration of Jewish law, compiled as guidelines for the Jewish people, between the second and fifth centuries A.D.

not deeply influenced by Greek thought, particularly that of Pythagoras, Plato, and the Academy.[15]

It is in this environment that the *Sefer Yetzirah* (The Book of Creation) is believed to have first emerged. It is a short treatise on ancient cosmology expressed in a Jewish framework, and there are several versions of it available in English. It well repays study, for the Sefer Yetzirah is recognised by most scholars as being the earliest and most important work on Kabbalah extant. There are different opinions concerning both its authorship and the date it was written. Traditionally it was attributed to Abraham himself; others think it a medieval creation. Gershom Scholem argues that it was probably composed in Palestine between the second and fourth centuries A.D.,[16] while Aryeh Kaplan, one of the great Jewish Kabbalists of recent times, suggests that it was in its present form as early as A.D. 204.[17]

FIFTH STAGE: THE ASCENDANCY OF CHRISTIANITY

In A.D. 315, Emperor Constantine transformed the world when he issued the Edict of Milan, legitimizing the long-persecuted Christian faith. In A.D. 323, after routing Licinius, Emperor of the East, Constantine gave Christianity preferential status in the empire. He also provided compensation for anyone who had been persecuted for their Christian beliefs, and furthermore, played an active role in promoting Christianity. He convened the Council of Nicaea (A.D. 325) to decide upon a theological dispute concerning the essence and nature of Christ, and to determine the order and organization of the church. He also sent a mission to Jerusalem with

---

15   Academy: The school in Athens established by Plato in the fourth century B.C. Its main objectives involved the philosophical education of men and their training for the service of Athens.

16   *Encyclopedia Judaica*, vol. 16, pp. 785–786.

17   Aryeh Kaplan, *Sefer Yetzirah* (York, ME: Weiser, 1990), p. xviii.

the purpose of discovering the site of the crucifixion, burial, and resurrection of Jesus. During his reign, Constantine set in motion a series of events that eventually led to the demise of the old religions and the closing of the mystery schools.

In A.D. 330 he transferred his court to Constantinople, his name for the rebuilt Byzantium. From the time of the Edict of Milan in A.D. 315, Constantine inaugurated an increasingly hostile policy towards paganism. This was maintained during the reign of his son, Constantine II, when more pressure was brought to bear against paganism. In A.D. 339, the Jews were forbidden to own Christian slaves, and the death penalty was instituted for those who took the Jewish faith. Marriages between Jews and Christians were forbidden on pain of death for any Jew who transgressed this law. As time passed, religions such as Judaism were either forced underground, to practise in secret, or to move to areas beyond the immediate influence of the administration. After A.D. 391, during the reign of Theodosius I (A.D. 379–395), Christianity became the new state religion and all other forms of religious expression were restricted and penalised within the increasingly Christian empire.

It should be understood, however, the essential spiritual teachings and philosophy of the ancient world did not fade into obscurity but were quietly absorbed by the Christian Church through the efforts of such men as Clement of Alexandria, Origen, St. Augustine, and the Pseudo-Dionysius. Indeed, the Christian philosophers of the third and fourth centuries completely took over the Neoplatonic system, adapting it to suit the growing intellectual framework of the Church. The hierarchy of the divine hypostases, as defined by Plotinus, was adapted to express the coequal nature of the Christian Trinity of God as Father, Son, and Holy Spirit, and the Platonic 'world of ideas' was integrated into the one supreme divine nature itself. This was clearly reflected in the ascetic disciplines of the Christian communities, particularly in the desert, where purification was sought not by separation, but through unification—the unification and transformation of the body, soul and spirit in Christ—which differed radically from the asceticism generally practised in the Greco-Roman world, which involved the use of psycho-spiritual processes designed to separate the soul from the body and its negative influence.

The influence of Greco-Roman philosophical thought, particularly Neoplatonism, also had a powerful effect upon the Jews in the form of the Diaspora, and its influence is to be seen in many important Kabbalistic works from the Sepher Yetzirah onward. The most influential figure among the Neoplatonists was undoubtedly Plotinus.[18] The essence of his teaching proposes three principal modes of being to which he applies the term 'hypostases' (see Table 1 below). The first he defines as The One, which is the prime source and principle of all being, the very ground of existence. The second is the Divine Nous or

Table 1. The Hypostases of Plotinus.

The One	The prime source and principle of all being, the ground of existence. It is the Good, the Infinite, the Absolute.
The Divine Nous	The divine spirit/mind in which exist the archetypal ideas and prototypes of creation.
The World Soul	Consists of a celestial part that contemplates the Divine Nous, and a terrestrial part through which it generates the material cosmos.

---

[18] Plotinus was born in Lycopolis in Egypt at the beginning of the third century. For more than ten years he studied philosophy at Alexandria under the guidance of his mentor Ammonius Saccas, eventually moving to Rome where he remained for the rest of his life. He published nothing, and as far as we know wrote only the various essays and lecture notes that constitute the substance of the *Enneads*. After his death his notes were edited and published by his student Porphyry.

Mind, in which exist the archetypal ideas and prototypes of all creation. The third, proceeding from the Divine Nous, is the World Soul, below which lies the realm of nature, which constitutes the outer life of the World Soul, and last of all there is undifferentiated matter, the last consequence of the outpouring of the One; it forms the lowest stage of the universe, and is thus understood to be the antithesis of the One.

The World Soul consists of two parts. First, a higher celestial part through which it contemplates the Divine Nous, and second, a lower terrestrial part, through which it generates the material cosmos according to the archetypal model contained within the Divine Nous. Human souls proceed from the World Soul, and like the World Soul may also be subdivided into two or more parts, for a human being, Plotinus taught, is a microcosm wherein the principles of the hypostases are reflected as spirit, soul and body (see Table 2 below). Below the sphere of the soul lies the material world, in which the soul's conjunction with matter and a material body takes place, and which Plotinus taught was a fall or descent from a higher state of being. It is from this fall or descent that the soul seeks redemption, and, to which Plotinus devotes much of his attention.

Table 2. The Human Macrocosm.

The Intuitive Soul	The realm of spiritual perception	Spirit
The Reasoning Soul	The realm of pure thought and discursive reasoning	Soul
The Unreasoning Soul	The realm of the psyche and the passionate nature.	Soul
The Material World	The realm of sensory perception	Body

Plotinus's model of the cosmos is significant in that he describes in literal terms what previously had been taught through metaphor and allegory and only experienced by the initiate during the celebration of the mysteries. At the centre of this celebration, with all of its pomp, ceremony, and drama, the consciousness of the initiate would have been elevated through the use of evocative prayer to experience the World Soul in the form of Demeter, and then after a different fashion, to experience the Divine Nous in the form of Dionysus. Plotinus believed that it was possible for individual souls, through the practise of contemplation, to ascend to the level of the Divine Nous, and there, in spiritual union, be absorbed back into the One. Plotinus describes the most important objectives of the mystery schools: the direct experience of, and union with, divinity. The first part, which may be thought of as the 'Lesser Mysteries', was concerned with the separation of the soul from the carnal nature of the physical body. The second part, which may be described as the 'Greater Mysteries', was essentially concerned with the elevation of the soul beyond the reactive nature of the psychic world into the presence of divinity where union could take place. Much of the Plotinus's thought is to be seen in later Kabbalistic thinking.

The Sixth Stage: The Talmud, Midrash, and the Rabbis

In this same period (second to fourth centuries), the Jewish people consolidated their faith in the wisdom of the rabbis who were successors to the Pharisees, and in the Talmud, which became the cultural benchmark for all Jews. In Palestine, during the second century, the oral teachings of the Jewish people were committed to writing, and consisted of two parts; firstly the *Halakha*, which embodies religious rites and ceremonies, civil and criminal law, and jurisprudence in general; and secondly, the *Haggada*, which consists of the thoughts, hopes, feelings, and wishes of the Jewish people as expressed in the customs, myths, parables, proverbs, and stories of the Torah.

The arrangement of this immense amount of material is in two forms; the first, known as the *Mishna*, is a compilation of laws and regulations. The second, known as the *Midrash*, is a collection of commentaries on, and discussions about, the books of the Torah. The Mishna, taken from Palestine to Babylon, was taught and explained in the schools founded there by the Palestinian Jews. These explanations, known as *Gemara*, consist of the records of discussions that took place in the Palestinian schools over the succeeding three centuries. In their contents they are a treasure house of everything that the most distinguished minds of Judaism of the period spoke, thought, felt, experienced, and knew. The Babylonian Gemara was completed about A.D. 500.

The Mishna (laws and regulations) and the Gemara (commentaries) together form the Talmud and, although not strictly a law book, the Talmud was eventually adopted as the only authority in matters of religious law, and, like the Mishna some 300 years previously, became the subject of great study and exposition. I labour this point to bring to your attention how important the Talmud and the commentaries that form the Midrash were to the Jewish people; and furthermore, how subsequent to the Roman destruction of Jerusalem the use of texts such as these have been fundamental to the development of Kabbalism.

The Seventh Stage: Byzantium and the Rise of Islam

From a non-Christian perspective, the rise of Islam in the seventh century was in some ways a stroke of good fortune. Islam, particularly in its early phase (A.D. 610–874), was very tolerant of other beliefs and absorbed, developed, and protected much of the philosophy and science of the ancient world. By the late seventh century, centres of learning had moved away from such places as Athens and Alexandria to new centres of learning such as Damascus, Cairo, and Baghdad. Thus for a very long period the Jews thrived under Islamic rule. In their unique way, both Byzantium and Islam proved to be fertile ground for the Tradition, particularly in its Neoplatonic form; this fact was to become apparent during the Western European Renaissance.

With the collapse of the Western Roman Empire, civilisation rapidly declined and much of Western Europe entered a long period of ignorance, war, poverty, and disease. The social structure of Roman civilisation was torn apart by invasion from without, and civil conflicts within. Education and the Arts fell by the wayside, to be maintained only by the Church. While Western Europe lay in the grip of these 'Dark Ages', the Eastern Roman Empire, centred around and named after the city and culture of Byzantium, flourished. By the sixth century, Byzantium had become the centre of civilisation in the declining Roman Empire, and was to remain an important centre of the civilised world until 1453 when it fell to the Turks. However, there were civilised areas of western Europe that were safe havens for the custodians of the Tradition. One such region was the Moorish territory in Spain. From the middle of the eighth until the middle of the eleventh century, the Moors ruled much of Spain from their capital Cordova. Their tolerant rule ensured a fruitful and luxuriant lifestyle for Muslim, Jew, and Christian alike.

Among the subjects of the ruling Caliphs were numerous Christian and Jewish communities forming an important part of the general economy. Together they constituted the principal channel through which the culture of Islam and Ancient Greece passed into the Latin world. This was particularly so in the bloody years of the late twelfth century when the tolerant rule of the Caliphs was overturned by the fierce Berbers of the Atlas mountains. The violent intolerance of these invaders drove many scholars and artisans from these communities into Christian territories.

Provence and the neighbouring region of Languedoc also tolerated different cultures and philosophies, making southern France an oasis of artistic and scientific excellence. The region supported not only the Cathars[19] but also a large international community of Jews, Arabs, Greeks, Spaniards, Italians, and Eastern Europeans, filling the intellectual environment with a dynamic mixture of Greco-Roman Neoplatonism, Dualism, and the esoteric teachings of Judaism, Christianity, and Islam. Here the Grail legends and the poetry of the troubadours reached their zenith, and, according to Scholem, the Kabbalah, as understood in modern times, was born.[20]

THE EIGHTH STAGE: THE EMERGENCE OF KABBALAH AS WE NOW UNDERSTAND IT

In Provence, during the late twelfth century, the *Sepher ha Bahir* (Book of Brilliance) first made its appearance. Apart from the *Sepher Yetzirah*, it is probably the oldest known Kabbalistic text, and is attributed to Rabbi Nehunyah ben ha-Kanah, master of a first-century esoteric school in Palestine. Its precise origin and authorship, however, are unknown.[21] From

---

[19] Catharism was a dualist form of Christianity that flourished in parts of western Europe, particularly in the region of Provence and Languedoc, during the twelfth and thirteenth centuries. Its doctrines resembled those of the Manicheans. It was condemned by the Church, and a crusade against the Cathars began in 1209. By the end of the thirteenth century, Catharism had effectively disappeared.

[20] Gershom Scholem, *Origins of Kabbalah* (Princeton: Princeton University Press, 1990), pp. 12–18.

[21] Gershom Scholem, *On the Kabbalah and Its Symbolism* (London: Routledge & Keegan Paul, 1965), p. 93.

the beginning of the thirteenth century Kabbalism began to emerge as a distinct spiritual movement that attained considerable prominence in southern France and Spain. It was out of this fertile hothouse of mystical speculation that not only the Bahir but also the Zohar (The Book of Splendour) were to emerge.

When the Roman Empire collapsed in the fifth century, western and eastern Europe went their separate ways, only to come together again in the centuries of the Crusades (A.D. 1095–1291). Whatever our opinion of the Crusades, the fact remains that because of them western European culture re-established its connections with the eastern empire and beyond. Through this contact a cultural renaissance took place that was to transform our world. This Renaissance, which is generally associated with fifteenth-century Florence, really began in the mid-twelfth century as a revival of classical Greco-Roman culture, although it was the fall of Constantinople in 1453 that precipitated the high point of the Renaissance, with Florence as its epicentre. Here, under the generous patronage of the Medici family, art, science, philosophy, and religion inspired by the ancient world of Greece and Rome and the contemporary cultures of Byzantium and Islam, flourished. Marsilio Ficino, with the support of Cosimo de' Medici, became the founder and inspiration of the Platonic Academy of Florence. As its name implies, it was dedicated to the study and translation of the works of Plato and the Academy of Athens. Ficino not only translated the works of Plato into Latin but also the works of Plotinus, Porphyry, Iamblichus, and Proclus, making available for the first time these classics of the ancient world to Christian scholars. In doing so, Ficino and the other members of the Academy also created the conditions by which the study of esoteric Judaism—that is Kabbalah—could be safely embraced in a sympathetic manner.

In the Christian world before the Protestant Reforma-tion[22] the Church authorities generally maintained a rigid control over what could be studied, taught, or published throughout Christendom. Anything that was deemed to contradict the authority of Scripture, or the enshrined teach-ings of the Church fathers and recognised doctors of the Church was viewed with intolerant suspicion and often sup-pressed. Speculative thought of a Jewish origin, particularly of a spiritual or philosophical nature, was invariably ignored in the intellectual circles of a prejudiced Christendom and often treated with hostility. This was in direct contrast to the emerging Florentine renaissance whose keynote, particularly in Italy, was tolerance. In such a climate, taboo subjects such as pagan religions and associated beliefs and practises were openly discussed. It was in this environment that the secret teachings of the Jewish mystics—the Kabbalah—entered upon the world stage.

The Ninth stage: The Kabbalah and the Renaissance

If Ficino was central to the renewal of interest in the classi-cal world of ancient Greece and Rome, then Giovanni Pico della Mirandola, a member of the Academy and perhaps Ficino's most notable disciple, was the key figure in draw-ing esoteric Judaic thought, in the form of Kabbalah, into the social limelight of Renaissance culture. His major work, *Nine Hundred Conclusions*, published in 1486, attempted to synthesise the mystical doctrines of Christianity with those of Judaism and Islam. Seventy-two of these conclusions were derived from Kabbalistic sources. This publication brought him into conflict with the Church authorities. He is also thought to have influenced Archangelus of Burgonovo, whose writings attempted to show how much the Jewish traditions

---

[22] The Reformation was a religious political and spiritual revolution in the western Church that began in 1517 when Martin Luther posted ninety-five theses on the door of the Palast Church in Wittenberg, Germany.

confirmed Christian traditions, and, the German Humanist Johann Reuchlin, whose book *De Arte Cabalistica*, published in 1517, is thought by some to be the beginning of Christian Kabbalah. Reuchlin's work, on the surface at least, tended toward the magical applications of Practical Kabbalah, and is thought to have greatly influenced the writings of Johann Trithemius and Heinrich Cornelius Agrippa.

In the midst of the Renaissance a body of work was published that has since mystified both Jew and non-Jew alike. This body of work is called the *Sefer Ha Zohar*, otherwise known as The Book of Splendour. The Zohar is the definitive work of Kabbalistic mysticism compiled, or perhaps composed, by Rabbi Moses de Leon in Spain during the late thirteenth century. For many years it was generally believed by both Jew and Christian alike that the Zohar was the work of Rabbi Simeon ben Yohai, a legendary figure of immense importance to the Tradition. Rabbi Simeon ben Yohai lived in first-century Palestine and, according to legend, he and his son retired into a secret cave for more than a dozen years, during which time the Zohar was alleged to have been written. However, the Zohar has now been identified as the work of Rabbi Moses de Leon, who lived and worked in Spain during the latter part of the thirteenth century. It was in circulation among Jewish esoteric circles in Spain and Provence for some considerable time before it found its way into Christian circles. In reality the Zohar is not a single unified work but is rather a great literary anthology consisting of several books that, in published editions, are generally divided into five parts that consist of esoteric commentaries and homiletics upon the Pentateuch and Jewish life in relation to Jewish scriptures. These parts are: 1) Genesis, 2) Exodus, 3) the rest of the Pentateuch, 4) Tikkunei Ha Zohar (Arrangements of the Zohar), and 5) Zohar Hadash (the New Zohar).

The Zohar was first printed in Hebrew in 1558–1560 as a three-volume edition in Mantua. At the same time a one-volume edition was published in Cremona. From the latter part of the sixteenth century onward, various translations appeared in both manuscript and printed form. However, the most significant translation was probably that of Christian Freiherr Knorr von Rosenroth (1636–1689), a German Kabbalist who translated the most important sections of the Zohar into Latin. This translation had a tremendous influence on Western thought, being the main source of information about the Zohar in cultured European circles until the beginning of the twentieth century.

THE TENTH STAGE: THE IMPACT OF KABBALAH ON THE REFORMATION

The Renaissance inspired the Reformation, the religious upheaval that commenced in earnest in the early years of the sixteenth century, and after long and bloody conflict eventually freed the Christian nations of western Europe from the decadent administration of Roman theocracy, which had for the best part of a thousand years endeavoured to suppress any religious views differing from the orthodox. Thus, throughout the sixteenth and seventeenth centuries this new freedom inspired in cultured circles a willingness to explore the spiritual teachings and philosophy of different religions—particularly esoteric Judaism in the form of Kabbalah—and so contributed in no small measure to a great flowering of spiritual thought. Luminaries such as Giorgio Francesco, Guillaume Postel, Robert Fludd, Heinrich Cornelius Agrippa, Athanasius Kircher, Jacob Boehme, Knorr von Rosenroth, Jane Lead, Henry More, Isaac Newton, William Law, Johann Valentin Andrea, Giordano Bruno, and Elias

Ashmole were all to some extent influenced by Kabbalistic thought. These and many more like them embodied the many different expressions of a very ancient tradition of spiritual evolution. This tradition, although not unique to Judaism, is most notably defined in the Jewish esoteric teachings that fall under the heading of Kabbalah.

The most remarkable thing about the Kabbalah is not so much that it outlines a tradition of spiritual development, but that it directed, and indeed continues to direct, observant Christians to the realization that within their own religious texts are to be found the very same esoteric tradition of spiritual development. Those who knew of this sought to inspire the world to rekindle the flames of the quest in the slumbering soul of our culture. They have left us a wonderful legacy, but unfortunately few people now understand it; we have yet again lost touch with what it means. This was particularly evident in the nineteenth and twentieth centuries, when 'hidden masters', 'secret chiefs', and 'transcendent adepts' led people *en masse* up the garden path. The advent of psychism (spiritualism, channelling, *etc*) witnessed the practise of blatant plagiarism, as the material of the Tradition was used to fulfil the ambitions of the naive and the unscrupulous.

At the beginning of this chapter I quoted Gershom Scholem, who defined Kabbalah as 'the sum of Jewish Mysticism'. Taking this definition literally, we must then accept the fact that Kabbalah was not invented in the thirteenth century, neither was it a Gnostic creation of the third or fourth century nor invented in pre-Christian Alexandria, or a by-product of the Babylonian captivity. The truth is simply what has always been claimed, that it is the secret doctrine of spiritual development that was transmitted through Moses to the people of Israel. In saying this I am not suggesting that it has remained unchanged ever since, as that would be preposterous. Obviously it has adapted and evolved to suit contemporary needs, particularly in the aforementioned areas. However, the basic premise remains that the essence of a unique process or method of spiritual development transmitted by Moses is still contained in the heart of Judaism, and furthermore, that heart is Kabbalah.

Chapter 2

The Basics of
Kabbalah

THE STUDY OF Kabbalah has generally been arranged by
different authors under several headings. S. L. Macgregor
Mathers, in the introduction to *The Kabbalah Unveiled* (his
translation of parts of Von Rosenroth's *Kabbalah Denudata*),
arranges the Kabbalah under the following four headings:

1. Practical Kabbalah, which deals with
    ceremonial and talismanic magic;
2. Literal Kabbalah, which deals with the
    use of language in different systems
    of codification and interpretation;
3. Unwritten Kabbalah, which deals
    with the oral teachings that are
    never entrusted to writing;
4. Dogmatic Kabbalah, which is essentially
    concerned with Kabbalistic doctrine.

Alternatively, in his book *The Kabbalah*, William Wynn
Westcott arranges the categories in much the same way as
Mathers, but uses two instead of four categories, these being:

1.   Practical Kabbalah;
2.   Dogmatic Kabbalah.

Under the heading of 'Practical Kabbalah', he includes all that Mathers incorporates in the Practical and Literal Kabbalah, and his category of dogmatic Kabbalah embraces the same doctrinal aspects of unwritten theoretical Kabbalah as defined by Mathers. Similarly, Isaac Myer states in *Qabbalah* that the Kabbalists of old divided their system into two main divisions:

1.   The Theoretic, which he divides
      into three branches: symbolic,
      speculative, and dogmatic;
2.   The Practical, which treats '... of angels
      and demons and their hierarchies and divi-
      sions, of the departments in Paradise and
      Hell, the transmigration of souls, etc'.[1]

Arthur Edward Waite, however, in his book *The Holy Kabbalah*, places the study of Kabbalah under four headings:

1.   Administrative Tradition (of the Talmud);
2.   Magical Tradition;
3.   Practical Kabbalah, which he describes
      as being concerned with the material
      Mathers associates with Literal Kabbalah;
4.   Philosophical Tradition, which is con-
      cerned with the teachings embodied
      in the Sefer Yetzirah and the Zohar.

This last category Waite portrays as the essential Kabbalah, which he describes as being concerned with two fundamen-

---

1   Isaac Myer, *Qabbalah* (San Diego: Wizard Bookshelf, 1988), p. 226.

tal doctrines: The Doctrine of Creation and the Doctrine of the Throne, or Chariot.[2]

In his book *Sefer Yetzirah*, Aryeh Kaplan states that Kabbalah may be divided into the following three categories:

1. Theoretical, which is concerned with the study of the Zohar;
2. Meditative, which is concerned with the use of divine names and the permutation of letters to attain heightened states of consciousness;
3. Magical, which is concerned with the use of signs, incantations, and the use of the divine names of God.[3]

The above authorities provide us with sufficient information to identify a basic pattern for the study of the Kabbalah. It is not difficult to perceive in the classifications outlined above that whichever scheme one uses the work will fall inevitably into two groups: The first is educational, the second practical—'theoria' and 'praxis'. The theoretical aspect of this work lies in the study of Scripture, commentaries upon it, Kabbalistic texts, and related material. The practical aspect of this work lies within the dynamic psycho-spiritual processes that are implicit within these texts. Both are subject to further division and both are dependent upon the scriptures.

Although there is some preparatory work that is accessible to anyone, there is no real beginning other than the study of the scriptures, especially the Mosaic books that compose the Pentateuch (the first five books of the Bible). Some might find this idea rather off-putting, but it should be borne in mind that the great Kabbalistic texts, the *Sefer Yetzirah*, the *Sefer ha Bahir*, and the *Sefer ha Zohar*, are all concerned with

---

2   Arthur Edward Waite, *The Holy Kabbalah* (New York: University Books, 1961), p. 37.

3   Aryeh Kaplan, *Sefer Yetzirah* (York Beach, ME: Weiser, 1990), p. x.

the revelation of an inner teaching embedded in the scriptures. It is this inner teaching, or tradition, that forms the essence of Kabbalah, and upon which the practical side of Kabbalah rests. Understand this one thing and all of the tools, methods, and systems of the Kabbalists—both ancient and modern—will then make sense. Furthermore, it is important to understand that the Kabbalah is not a single unique and uniform system and philosophy shared by all Kabbalists. There have been, and there continue to be, different schools of thought concerning the interpretation and application of the principles involved. Some of the earlier exponents were more philosophical, inclining toward a rational interpretation while others, including the authors of the Zoharic literature, favoured a mythological approach.

The literal interpretation of Scripture is undoubtedly valuable and should not be set aside as one seeks to understand the inner teaching; for the literal interpretation teaches us a way of living in harmony with God's law, with each other, and with our conscience. It contains a code for living a wholesome life that constitutes the platform for the more subtle work of the spirit. Sadly, rather than seeking the spiritual treasures hidden within it, many people have preferred to seek codes and ciphers that might reveal material treasures and knowledge of great secrets, and doubtless many more will lead themselves up the same garden path in search of the same. Yet, there is more; there are ciphers, which are very difficult to crack, there are treasures far greater than fame or fortune, and there are secrets. The question is, how does one find them and how does one understand them? The simple truth is that the answer lies in where you direct your attention. A famous Kabbalist of the seventeenth century, Menasseh ben Israel, compared the Mosaic books to the body of a human being, the commentaries on them such as the Zohar, he likened to the soul, and the Kabbalah he compared to the spirit of the soul: ignorant people, he taught, may study the first, the learned may study the second, but the wise, he said, direct their contemplation to the third.

Another Kabbalist, Nicholas de Lyra, a Christian scholar who died in 1340, recognised four modes of interpretation: literal, allegorical, moral, and anagogic or mystical. Moses de Leon (d. 1305) taught that the word *Pardes* (PaRDeS), which means 'garden' or 'paradise' is a cipher concealing an esoteric understanding of existence based upon four levels of interpretation. He taught that each consonant of the word PaRDeS denotes one of four levels of interpretation and meaning. Thus: P stands for the literal meaning; R stands for the allegorical meaning in the moral sense; D stands for the allegorical in the symbolic sense; S stands for the mystical meaning.[4]

Arthur Edward Waite described the same thing thus; P equals the literal, R the symbolic, D the allegorical, and finally S equals the mystical sense.[5] This method of interpretation applies particularly to the life of the soul on its path of spiritual regeneration, not to political or historical secrets and intrigues. On this path the Torah—that is the Pentateuch, the first five books of the Old Testament—play an essential role, and must be interpreted according to this method, which was likened by Moses de Leon to a nut with a shell of literal meaning on the outside and an essence or mystical meaning within. To the Kabbalist the Torah does not consist simply of meaningful ancient records and teachings arranged into chapters and sections: rather, it is understood to be the living incarnation of divine wisdom, the symbolic embodiment of the creative powers of God. The physical Torah is a representation of that wisdom; each letter, each word, representing a spiritual dimension of life open to the righteous soul, and as such it is capable of being a vehicle of almost infinite knowledge.

---

4   Scholem, *On the Kabbalah and Its Symbolism*, p 57.

5   Waite, *The Holy Kabbalah*, p. 198.

With this in mind all of the great Kabbalists have accepted as a given that the study of the Scriptures is absolutely necessary for spiritual progress. However, merely reading such texts does not make a Kabbalist. The practical work of a Kabbalist involves a serious and prolonged engagement with the interior life of the soul, especially in its relationship with God, and it is to this interior life that Kabbalah is dedicated. Therefore, it is not possible for an atheist or an agnostic to become a Kabbalist; nor should such a person attempt such work for there are dangerous hazards involved not only for the impious but also for the curious and foolhardy. Furthermore, any who think that the magical or meditative categories are all that they need, fail to understand that the coarseness of human consciousness, however refined we may think it to be, is insufficient for any real progress in this work. In addition, without spiritual assistance, they will fail to comprehend the essential nature and chemistry of their consciousness, which is the main theatre of their work; thus, they will be doomed to failure because the work of the Kabbalist is, in essence, the work of spiritual regeneration, which is not primarily a process of elevating consciousness to 'higher worlds', but the transformation of the very essence of consciousness itself.

THE VEILS OF NEGATIVE EXISTENCE

The mystical doctrines of the Kabbalah, like those of the mystical doctrines of all cultures, have had to address the problem of reconciling the absolute nature of God with the imperfect nature of creation. If God is so absolutely singular, self-contained and perfect, then how does an apparently imperfect creation come into existence; how does the infinite bring the finite into being, and as a finite being, how does humanity in its imperfect state have any comprehension of

God? In response to these questions; and to demonstrate the separateness of creation from God, the early Kabbalists proposed three stages or states prior to the act of creation. The first stage is based upon the premise that before the 'Beginning', before the creation of the Universe there was Nothing—no Space, no Time, no Energy, no Dimension, no Activity, no Purpose or Existence, in fact Nothing! This absolute the Kabbalist calls AIN—'Nothingness'. It is a term that signifies the Godhead in its most impenetrable guise. It is therefore a symbol of a mystery concerning the nature of the source of existence; a mystery that is completely beyond the grasp of human intellect.

From this mystery of Nothingness, early Kabbalists proposed the presence of a hidden something, an infinite Godhead. The Kabbalist calls this hidden Godhead AIN SOPH—'the Boundless'—a term that represents an invisible and undifferentiated Godhead, in whom absolute potential and perfection consists. When referred to as a divine entity, however mysterious, it is more often referred to as *En-Sof*, and I shall use the latter term from this point on. The teachings of the Kabbalah maintain that En-Sof does not reveal itself in any 'finite' way; it is not even accessible to the innermost thought of the contemplative. Yet from this divine Godhead—who is the first cause, the One of Plotinus—the entire creation emanates.

Concerning the emanation of creation, they taught that En-Sof contracted a space within itself and filled it with an infinite and boundless light. This infinite ocean of divine light the Kabbalist calls AIN SOPH AUR—'Infinite Light'. Kabbalistic doctrine maintains that En-Sof concentrated this light into a central point, a point of infinite potential, a point that is known as Kether, and from which emanates the powers and potencies by which the universe is brought into existence; and in which the hidden Godhead is revealed as the creator of the universe and controller of its destiny. These potencies and powers, including Kether, are known as the ten Sephiroth—the fundamental components of the Tree of Life

Kether is then the title by which the first expression of the divine will as positive existence is known. It is Unity itself, and as such is incomparable for there is nothing with which to compare it. It is the source of all things, the very wellspring of life and existence—ever the seed, ever the source, the focal point of life itself. It is the First Point, the first cause of existence, and as such it is the antecedent of duality and all that

1.   AIN   Nothingness
2.   AIN SOPh   Boundless
3.   AIN SOPh AUR   Infinite Light

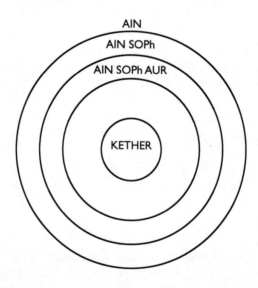

Fig. I. The Veils of Negative Existence.

plies. Kether is effectively synonymous with En-
~ strictly speaking it is impossible to refer directly to
~hat is available is what can be inferred, thus: if Kether
~ntecedent of duality it must be without form; being
~oreal it must be without body, and being beyond time
it transcends generation and gender. Furthermore, it is also
taught that Kether, as Unity, is present in all created things,
animate and inanimate, in the sense that it is the substrate of
existence. Thus it is said that the name that applies to Kether
is I Am That I Am. It is from Kether that the entire creation,
traditionally represented as a tree, springs forth. This tree is
diagrammatically portrayed as a geometrical arrangement of
ten spheres, or Sephiroth.

THE TREE OF LIFE AND THE TEN SEPHIROTH

The tree has been a key symbol in the life of humanity from
the earliest times. The reverence in which the tree is held is
evident in every culture and civilisation that has kept records
of its history. To the ancient Egyptians, the universal Tree of
Life was a colossal tree that served as the central axis of the
cosmos, on the summit of which perched the Phoenix, the
symbol of immortality. The sycamore tree was often used as
a representation of the Tree of Life from within which the
goddess Nut dispensed the drink of immortality, and the fruit
that imparted the knowledge of good and evil, thus enabling
the discriminating soul to reach the fields of Amentet.[6]

According to Scandinavian mythology, the ash tree
Yggdrasil is the greatest of all trees; it is the world tree that
holds together heaven, earth, and the underworld. Nine
worlds are believed to be contained within it. At its roots is
a fountain of sacred water that has the powers of purification and regeneration. It has three main roots, beneath the

---

6   Amentet is the name of the underworld—the place where the sun sets,
which is the entrance to the underworld. Also, a goddess who personified
the Land of the West and welcomed the deceased into the underworld.

first is to be found the realm of the frost giants, beneath the second the realm of man, and beneath the third the realm of hell. One description speaks of a great cockerel, glittering like gold, standing upon its highest branch, another says that perched upon its highest branch is a great eagle, between whose eyes sits a hawk.[7]

In Hinduism the tree is generally considered to be a symbol of universal life and immortality. However, to those living the mystical life, it is a manifestation of the god Brahma, with the rest of the gods forming its branches. It is said to grow in Brahma's world in the midst of the lake Ara, from which the waters of eternal youth are drawn. It has many names, but as the Soma Tree, the world tree furnishes the divine ambrosia, or essence of immortality. The Asvattha Tree, the sacred tree in Buddhism, imparts wisdom and produces the divine ambrosia—the food of immortality; and furthermore, provides a dwelling for the souls of the blessed.[8] Under the Asvattha Tree, the Buddha sat and went through different stages of consciousness, until he attained enlightenment and received the knowledge of the sources of mortal suffering. The world tree of the ancient Iranians, the Haoma, produces the primal drink of immortality after which it is named. It is the first of all trees, planted by Ormuzd in heaven, in the fountain of life. It is protected by ten fish, who keep a ceaseless watch upon a lizard, or dragon, sent by the evil Ahriman, to destroy the sacred tree.

The Judeo-Christian scriptures describe the original home of humanity as a 'Garden of Delight' placed eastward in Eden.[9] Of this it is written that in the midst of the Garden are to be found two trees; one is the Tree of Knowledge of Good and Evil, and the other, the Tree of Life. Of the

---

[7]   J. A. MacCulloch, *Mythology of all Races, vol 2: Eddic* (New York: Cooper Square, 1964), p. 331.

[8]   Richard Folkard, *Plant Lore, Legends, and Lyrics* (London: Sampson Low, Marston & Co., 1892), p. 4-5.

[9]   Genesis 2:8–17.

Fig. 2. Yggdrasil—the Scandinavian World Tree (originally published in Finn Magnusen's *Eddalaeren*, reprinted in J. H. Philpot, *The Sacred Tree*, 1897).

former we are informed that in eating its fruit, Adam and Eve defied God's will and were consequently driven out of Paradise into a life of mortality and suffering; whereas, it is said of the Tree of Life, that whosoever eats of its fruit gains immortality—the never-ending quest of mankind. It is not surprising then, that one of the principal conceptions of Kabbalistic thought is the Tree of Life, as a macro and microcosmic model of creation. One of the earliest published diagrams of the Kabbalistic Tree of Life appeared in 1516 on the title page of *Portae Lucis*, a Latin translation of a Kabbalistic work written by Rabbi Joseph Gikatilla. It is now available in English under the title *Gates of Light*.[10] However, it is the diagram of Athanasius Kircher, first published in his magnum opus *Oedipus Aegyptiacus* (1652–1654), that is most familiar to non-Jewish Kabbalists.

There are many variations of the layout of the Tree of Life, the majority of which conform to an arrangement of ten spheres, or Sephiroth, and twenty-two paths connecting them (see figure 3 on page 37). The earliest description of the Sephiroth and the twenty-two paths occurs in the Sepher Yetzirah, a text which was once attributed to the patriarch Abraham, but is now understood to be the work of Simeon ben Yohai, the great Jewish sage who lived in Palestine in the second century. It describes a metaphysical system that lies at the heart of a prophetic science of the stars and is probably deeply rooted in the astral religions of ancient Egypt and Mesopotamia. The following quotation from the Sefer Yetzirah is often used as the basis for the Tree of Life:

> In thirty-two mysterious Paths of Wisdom did Jah the Jehovah of hosts, the God of Israel, the Living Elohim, the King of ages, the merciful and gracious God, the Exalted One, the Dweller in eternity, most high and holy—engrave his name by the three Sepharim—Numbers, Letters and Sounds. Ten are the ineffable Sephiroth. Twenty-two are the Letters, the Foundation of all things; there are Three Mothers, Seven Double and Twelve Simple letters. The ineffable Sephiroth are ten, as are the Numbers; and as there are in man five fingers over against five, so over them is established a covenant of strength, by word of mouth, and by the circumcision of the flesh. Ten is the number of the ineffable Sephiroth, ten and not nine, ten and not eleven. Understand this wisdom, and be wise by the perception. Search out concerning it, restore the Word to its creator, and replace Him who formed it upon his throne.

---

[10]　Weistein, trans., *Gates of Light* (New York: Harper Collins, 1994).

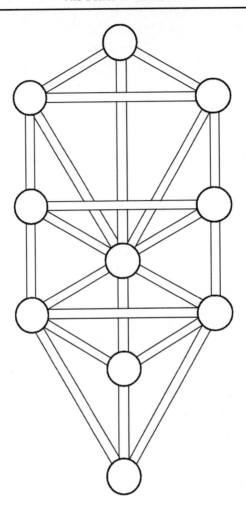

Fig. 3. The Tree of Life with paths.

> The Ten ineffable Sephiroth have ten vast regions
> bound unto them; boundless in origin and having
> no ending; an abyss of good and of ill; measure-
> less height and depth; boundless to the East and
> the West; boundless to the North and South; and
> the Lord the only God, the Faithful King, rules
> all these from his holy seat, for ever and ever.[11]

If the Sephiroth were first referred to in the Sepher Yetzirah,
it was the Sepher ha Bahir that demonstrated their pre-
eminence. Indeed, much of the terminology used in the
Bahir is now part of the mainstream vocabulary of Kabbalah.
Thus, in the teachings of Rabbi Isaac the Blind[12] we find for
the first time the Kabbalistic system of the ten Sephiroth
being used in the manner adopted by subsequent Kabbalists.
Rabbi Isaac taught that the Sephiroth are expressions of
divine will which preceded the physical heaven and physical
earth. According to Gershom Scholem,

> The ten *Sefiroth* constitute the mystical Tree of God
> or tree of divine power each representing a branch
> whose common root is unknown and unknowable.
> But *En-Sof* is not only the hidden Root of all Roots,
> it is also the sap of the tree; every branch represent-
> ing an attribute, exists not only by itself but by virtue
> of *En-Sof*, the hidden God. And this tree of God is
> also, as it were, the skeleton of the universe; it grows
> throughout the whole of creation and spreads its
> branches through all its ramifications. All mundane
> and created things exist only because something of
> the power of the *Sefiroth* lives and acts in them.[13]

---

[11] W. W. Westcott, *Sepher Yetzirah*, in *Collectanea Hermetica* (York, ME:
Weiser, 1998) pp. 15-16.

[12] Rabbi Isaac the Blind ca. 1165–1235, son of the rabbi Abraham ben
David of Posqueres (Spain). Isaac is often described as the 'Father of the
Kabbalah'.

[13] Gershom Scholem, *Major Trends in Jewish Mysticism* (New York:
Schocken Books, 1946), pp. 214–215.

Scholem articulates beautifully a fundamental principal of Kabbalistic teaching, which is that the entire creation and all things within it, especially man, were constructed on the pattern of the Sephiroth. They are the divine archetypes of existence in which it is understood that the designs for all the worlds were sketched, and which serve as patterns for creation. It follows, then, that the appropriate contemplation of creation will reveal the divine archetypes reflected therein, and it is taught in some circles that when the soul is purified, the locked gates of the world of Emanation will open, allowing the soul to enter.

As cosmological symbols, the Sephiroth express ten extremes or polarities in a three-dimensional world: up, down, east, west, north, south (space), beginning and end (time), good and evil (moral dimension). However, from a theological perspective they are channels, vehicles, or vessels through which the will of the divine En-Sof[14] is made manifest, an invisible superstructure upon which the entire creation hangs. Most Kabbalists do not regard the Sephiroth as existing outside the realm of the Godhead—that is to say, as spiritual intermediaries between God and man— and in this sense they are fundamentally distinct from the Neoplatonic conception of the hypostases which are perceived as being, as it were, hierarchical stages between the infinite and the finite, between the One and the Many. The Sephiroth, on the other hand, are spiritual forces of equal status and value existing in the Godhead; they themselves cannot be known, but the influence that flows from them reflects the life of the Godhead into the whole of creation. Therefore, they may be understood as spiritual forces governing and directing the cosmos and reflected in man as attributes of the soul.

---

[14] In Kabbalistic teaching Creation is bound up with the manifestation of the hidden God who is known as En-Sof.

Kether

Fig. 4. Kether
on the Tree of Life

The Sephiroth are perceived as emanating from En-Sof in succession, like one candle being lit from another, yet, without detracting anything from their source or from each other in any way. The first of the Sephiroth is Kether. To the Kabbalist, Kether is to all intents and purposes synonymous with En-Sof, except with this distinction, it is the first point of positive existence, a term that signifies the first germ of the creative process emerging out of the Godhead. Conceptually it is as a seed, in which the entire plan of creation resides and from which creation springs, and upon which creation depends; however, because it is pre-creation, Kether is unknowable and inaccessible to all created beings, including the human mind. Nothing can be attributed to it that can be described in terms of duality; it is the essence of Unity and all that such implies.

Nevertheless, Kabbalists have attributed to Kether certain sublime and ineffable qualities, and have ascribed to it many names or titles that embody such qualities in different ways. One is 'Kether Elyon', The Crown, for it is understood that Kether is as a crown to the divine archetypal man, Adam Kadmon. Another is *Eheieh*, which translates as 'I Am That I Am', the self-existent and self-begotten source of all that is and ever will be. 'The Inscrutable Height' is another title that defines Kether's inaccessibility to the human mind. The term 'Macroprosopus', the Great Countenance, describes Kether as the revealed aspect of the Hidden God, about which the Zohar has much to say. The title 'White Head' alludes to the brilliance of Kether as the head of the Macroprosopus. Other titles one may come across are: Ancient of Ancients; Concealed of the concealed; Ancient of Days; The Primordial Point and The Ancient One. There are many more titles used by different schools to describe the sublime nature of Kether, but if there is one thing that most Kabbalists attribute to Kether it is Will, the Will of the Godhead embodied in the first point of positive existence.

Chokmah

The second Sephira is Chokmah, a word that translates as 'Wisdom'. It represents the first dynamic act in the process of creation emanating out of Kether. It signifies the advancement of the Will of God and contains within itself the essence of the succeeding Sephiroth and the plan or blueprint of creation. It is the masculine power of

Fig. 5. Chokmah
on the Tree of Life

the divine, the father of all that will be. To it is attributed the letter Yod, the first letter of the Tetragrammaton (see page 62).

Binah

Out of Chokmah emanates Binah (see figure 6, page 42), the third Sephira, which translates as 'Intelligence' or 'Understanding'. It is the second dynamic act of the Godhead, and corresponds to the concept of a builder who receives

the blueprint and gives form to the designs thereon. It is the feminine power of the divine, the mother of all that will be. To it is attributed Hé, the second letter of the Tetragrammaton.

The Supernals

Fig. 6. Binah
on the Tree of Life

The first three Sephiroth are known as the 'Three Supernals'; they represent a progression from Will to the inception and formation of the ideal. These Sephiroth cannot be realised, even with specialised training in meditation techniques, for they transcend all activities of human consciousness. They constitute the well-spring of creation and are separated from the lower Sephiroth by a great abyss; on one side of which is Unity and the Ideal, and on the other diversity and the substantial.

Thus, symbolism is generally employed in Kabbalah to express the nature of the profound realities involved. What is more, the symbolism employed is frequently basic and necessarily universal. Thus, Chokmah—the Supernal Father, sows his seed in the womb of Binah—the Supernal Mother, who gives birth to the succeeding Sephiroth—the basic principles of creation. Another description portrays Chokmah as *Spiritus Primus* and Binah as *Materia Prima*; the combination of one with the other producing the living universe that we inhabit. Another emblematic representation describes Binah as the root of a tree nourished by the waters of Chokmah. This tree has seven branches (Sephiroth) that form the basis of creation. What must be born in mind with such symbolism is that the Sephirotic realm is a spiritual

realm far beyond the comprehension of this world; therefore, metaphor and allegory are not only useful, but essential
tools for describing such spiritual realities.

That the Sephiroth are real to the Kabbalist is unde-
niable, but they are real within the Godhead and must
not be confounded with material things. Thus, what is
described as a relationship between Chokmah and Binah
is an internal chemistry of the one thing, out of which
emerges the multitude of the 'many'; and to the Kabbalist
the 'many' are the next seven Sephiroth and everything
arising from them. Furthermore, each Sephira has a
positive or masculine potency to the Sephira following
it and a negative or feminine potency to the Sephira preceding it. This means that with the exception of Kether
and Malkuth all of the Sephiroth have a dual nature in
relationship to each other. Consequently the symbolism
involved is often extremely complex and not all that it
seems. Psychoanalysis, however, is never a useful tool for
understanding Kabbalistic symbolism.

Chesed

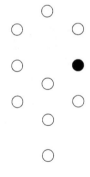

Emanating from Binah is
the fourth Sephira, Chesed,
which means 'love' or
'mercy'; It is the first of six
Sephiroth that constitute the
Lesser Countenance, or the
Microprosopus. As such it is
associated with the first development of three-dimensional
existence and the transfor-

Fig. 7. Chesed
on the Tree of Life

mation of archetypal forms into material expression. Thus
it is written 'Chesed shall build up forever'.[15] Now one of

---

15 Psalm 89:2.

the main attributions of Chesed is 'love' and it is by love and through love that creation is built; for the motives and intentions of God are beautiful, noble and sane; therefore the universe was created by God as an act of love. In human terms, Chesed corresponds with kindness and compassion. Another name for Chesed is Gedulah, which translates as 'greatness' or 'magnificence'. To it are attributed the divine name EL, the Mighty One, and the element of water.

Geburah

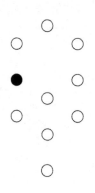

Fig. 8. Geburah
on the Tree of Life

Emanating from Chesed is Geburah, the fifth Sephira. Geburah means 'strength', or 'severity'. Whereas Chesed demonstrates the boundless outpouring of God's, love Geburah represents the control and regulation of that outpouring. In much the same manner that Chokmah and Binah balance each other, so do Geburah and Chesed, of whom it is said too much mercy is weakness and too much severity is cruelty and the ebbing away of the will. Another name for Geburah is *Din*, which means 'justice', thus, Geburah is the Sephira of justice, controlling and regulating the forces of the lower seven Sephiroth. In human terms it corresponds to discrimination. To Geburah are attributed the divine name ELOHIM GIBOR, the sphere of Mars, and the element of fire.

Tiphereth

The sixth Sephira is Tiphereth (see figure 9 on page 45), which means 'beauty' or 'mildness'. It is the centre of the

entire Tree and attributed to
it is Vau, the third letter of
the Tetragrammaton, and the
title *Zauir Anpin*—the Lesser
Countenance. Tiphereth is
a lower reflection of Kether
manifested through Chokmah
and Binah, and whose body
consists of the Sephiroth
Chesed, Geburah, Tiphereth,
Netzach, Hod, and Yesod.
These six Sephiroth form two
triads, an upper and a lower;

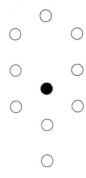

Fig. 9. Tiphereth
on the Tree of Life

in the upper triad, Tiphereth unites the forces of Chesed
and Geburah—love and strength, balancing and harmonizing them to establish a perfect equilibrium throughout the entire Tree. Tiphereth is the *Logos* (see Glossary),
which mediates between the upper and lower worlds of the
Sephirotic realm; within it is to be found the archetypal
forms that constitute the unseen superstructure of our universe. It is the sum of all goodness revealed in the form of
the perfect ideal, Adam Kadmon, who gives life and sustenance to all creatures in every world. He is the king and
Malkuth is his queen. To Tiphereth are attributed the divine
name ELOAH VADAATH, the Archangel Raphael and the
sphere of the Sun.

Netzach, Hod, and Yesod

The lower triad of the Lesser Countenance consists of
Netzach, Hod, and Yesod. The name Netzach means 'victory'
or 'endurance', Hod means 'splendour' or 'glory', and Yesod
means 'foundation'. Together Netzach and Hod form, as it
were, the two arms of God. They constitute the base of the

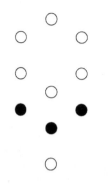

pillars of Mercy and Severity (see figure 13, p. 50) channelling the influx of the creative powers of all that is above. The Zohar says of them, 'All the energies, forces and increase to the universe, proceed through them'.[16] The combined output of Netzach and Hod unite in one harmonious vessel, Yesod, the foundation and basis of all generation. To Netzach are attributed the divine

Fig. 10. Netzach, Hod, and Yesod on the Tree of Life

name of YHVH TzBAOTh, the Lord of Hosts, the Archangel Haniel and the sphere of Venus. To Hod are attributed the divine name of ELOHIM TzABAOTh, the God of Hosts, the Archangel Michael, and the sphere of Mercury. To Yesod are attributed the divine name of SHADDAI EL CHAI, the Mighty Living God, the Archangel Gabriel, and the sphere of the Moon. This triad represents the material world in all its diversity, but it is not as yet manifest in the physical

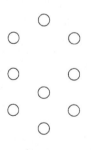

forms that are so apparent to our senses. It consists, rather, of a subtle energy that forms the matrix to which all things in the physical world conform and take their shape.

Malkuth

The final Sephira is Malkuth—the Kingdom. Emanating from Yesod, it is the final outcome, the last stage of

Fig. 11. Malkuth on the Tree of Life

---

16   Isaac Myer, *Qabbalah: The Philosophical Writings of Solomon Ben Yehudah Ibn Gebirol* (San Diego: Wizard's Bookshelf, 1988), p. 201.

Creation. It is the sum total of the creative activity of the preceding Sephiroth and represents the establishment of the Kingdom of God. To it is attributed Hé, the last letter of the Tetragrammaton. As the final Sephirah, Malkuth is naturally feminine and receptive, receiving the influx of the energies of all the preceding Sephiroth. Thus Malkuth is represented in the scriptures by symbols of the feminine principle of Binah, such as the matriarchs of the Pentateuch—especially Rachel and Leah, the wives of Jacob, a masculine principle of Tiphereth. Malkuth is also represented by Bathsheba, whose name in Hebrew means 'Daughter of Seven', that is, of the lower seven Sephiroth. On the other hand, although Malkuth is feminine in relationship to the other Sephiroth, it is also masculine in relationship to the worlds beneath itself (our world being one of these worlds). Thus Malkuth is also represented by King David, and the union of King David and Bathsheba represents the union of the positive and negative principles of Malkuth, the symbolism of which alchemists have speculated on a great deal.

However, we must avoid thinking that Malkuth is the material world of the senses as we know and experience it, for such thinking is fundamentally wrong. The Sephirotic World is not the creation but the spiritual basis of the creation; and the Sephiroth are the divine archetypes that serve as patterns for the entire cosmos; thus Malkuth is the pattern for this world in which we have so much of our existence. Malkuth is known to the Kabbalist as, Bride of Microprosopus, Queen Matrona, Inferior Mother, and the Shekinah (in Exile). Attributed to Malkuth are the divine name ADONAI HA ARETz, the Archangel Sandalphon and the sphere of the Elements. The Sephiroth are named as follows (see figure 12 on page 48):

1. Kether   כתר
2. Chokmah   חכמה
3. Binah   בינה
4. Chesed   הסד
5. Geburah   גבירה
6. Tiphereth   תפארת
7. Netzach   נצח
8. Hod   הוד
9. Yesod   יסיד
10. Malkuth   מלכות

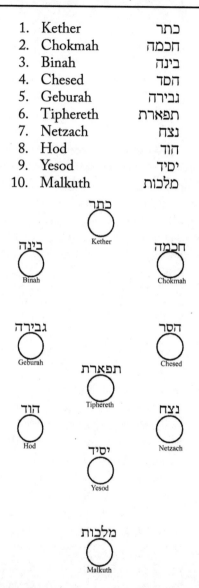

Fig. 12. Names of the Sephiroth.

THE PILLARS

The Sephiroth may also be viewed as three columns or pillars (see figure 13 on page 50). The central pillar extends from Kether to Malkuth, the left-hand pillar from Binah to Hod and the right-hand pillar from Chokmah to Netzach. It is apparent that these pillars depict the potencies of the Three Supernals in extension. The left-hand pillar is known as the Pillar of Judgement (or Severity), receiving its name from the Sephira Geburah (Judgement or Severity). It expresses the feminine quality of Binah which is known as *Aima*, the Supernal Mother. The right-hand pillar is known as the Pillar of Mercy, receiving its name from the Sephira Chesed (Mercy). It expresses the masculine quality of Chokmah, which is also known as *Abba*, the Supernal Father. The central pillar is neutral and androgynous; it receives the natures of both pillars and combines them in the Unity that is the essential attribute of Kether.

The Pillar of Judgement consists of three Sephiroth: Binah, Geburah, and Hod. To the Sephira of Binah is ascribed understanding, to Geburah, judgement (sometimes fear), to Hod, splendour or glory. The Pillar of Mercy consists of the three Sephiroth, Chokmah, Chesed, and Netzach. To Chokmah is attributed wisdom, to Chesed, mercy, and to Netzach, victory (or endurance). The middle pillar, the Pillar of Mildness, consists of the four Sephiroth: Kether, Tiphereth, Yesod, and Malkuth. Among other considerations these Sephiroth denote states of soul consciousness that may be understood thus: Malkuth represents the soul's consciousness of the material world via the senses; it is invariably an instinctive and reactive state. Yesod corresponds to the interior psychic realm of the imagination; it is an astral world of images, dreams, and fantasies and is invariably appetitive and reactive. Tiphereth represents the place of self-consciousness; it is the realm of pure thought devoid of images and sensation,

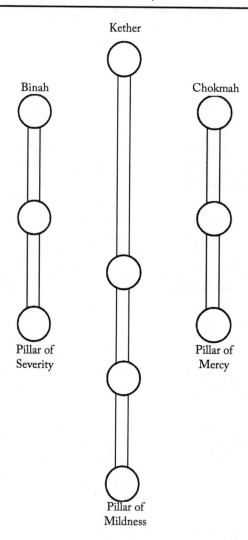

Fig. 13. The Pillars of the Tree of Life.

although in an unregenerate state it is invariably subject to desire and ambition, and as such exists in a world of moral conflict between personal desire and social obligation. It is here that the mystic realises the ephemeral nature of desire and learns to surrender the human will to the spiritual will of the Divine. At the summit of the middle pillar is Kether, the wellspring of all existence, the source and destiny of life.

Although in principle separate, the left and right hand pillars operate in conjunction with each other to define the dynamics of polarity that are fundamental components of duality. Because of them we experience space and time, male and female, form and generation, life and death, positive and negative, light and darkness, hot and cold, *etcetera*. The potencies of the two pillars are harmonised in and by the middle pillar, which is both their centre of gravity and the pole around which they orbit. The middle pillar is known as the Pillar of Mildness. In Kabbalah, the aspirant learns to identify the nature and influences of the left and right-hand pillars, to see them as factors influencing behaviour and conditioning perception. Having identified them, the aspiring mystic may then proceed to develop the ability to shape or modify behaviour according to the principles of the middle pillar—the Pillar of Mildness. It is axiomatic in Kabbalistic schools that too much severity is cruelty, and too much mercy is weakness and the ebbing away of the will. This rule, applied at each level of the Pillar of Mildness is an aid to the evolving soul on its path of spiritual regeneration.

There are other attributes to the pillars: to Geburah is attributed the left arm and to Chesed the right arm. It is said that, 'the right arm draws the immensity of space in love; the left arm draws the immensity of space in rigour'.[17] To Hod is attributed the left hip and to Netzach the right hip. In some quarters, the four rivers of Eden are attributed to Chesed, Geburah, Netzach, and Hod; the middle pillar is likened to

---

17   Waite, *The Holy Kabbalah*, p. 202.

the Tree of Life and the other pillars to the Tree of Knowledge of Good and Evil.

There is a connection between these pillars and the two pillars that were set up in front of the sanctuary in King Solomon's Temple.[18] The description of the building of the temple is in itself a study in sacred geometry. In Kabbalistic terms, however, the temple is the interior of the soul. Its outer courtyard is Malkuth, and it was divided into two; the first part was known as the People's Court, the second as the Priest's Court. The symbolism here is very revealing. Yesod is the Sanctuary, often described as the Holy Place, at the entrance of which stand the Pillars, known as Jachin and Boaz. Within the depths of the Holy Place lies the entrance to the Holy of Holies, the inner sanctum of the Temple, which on the Tree of Life is Tiphereth. The entrance to the inner temple is then through harmonizing the forces of the two pillars, the Pillar of Mercy, corresponding with Jachin, and the Pillar of Judgement, which corresponds with Boaz. The middle pillar, the Pillar of Mildness, is none other than the aspiring mystic, who must first overcome the world of the senses in order to enter the inner temple.

THE FOUR WORLDS

If the Sephiroth represent the powers and potencies by which En-Sof is revealed, then the whole Sephirotic realm is a representation of En-Sof in the form of the Tree of Life. However, this realm is an invisible realm inaccessible to the human mind, and would remain so if it were not made manifest through a process of graduated emanation. Thus, the Tree of Life may be recognised and understood in four increasingly material modes with distinct qualities and attributes. These four modes are described as four worlds or levels of Divine expression and manifestation:

---

18   See I Kings 7: 5–22, 41–42 and II Chron. 3:15–17; 4:12–13.

Atziluth	The archetypal world
Briah	The creative world
Yetzirah	The formative world
Assiah	The material world

It is possible to regard these four worlds as the Sephirotic Tree (figure 14 on page 55) thus: The first world is Atziluth, the World of Emanation, to which are attributed the Sephiroth Kether, Chokmah, and Binah. From this world emerge in succession the remaining three worlds: Briah, the World of Creation, to which are attributed the Sephiroth Chesed, Geburah, and Tiphereth; Yetzirah, the World of Formation, to which are attributed the Sephiroth Netzach, Hod, and Yesod; finally, Assiah, the World of Making, which consists of Malkuth alone. It is also possible to envisage the whole Sephirotic Tree as the archetypal model for each of the four worlds, concerning which it is written in Isaiah, 'Everyone who is *called* by my name, whom I have *created* for my glory; I have *formed* him, yes, I have *made* him'.[19] Thus, to the world of Atziluth are attributed the words, 'Everyone who is *called* by my name', signifying that this is the world in which En-Sof manifests in the form of the archetypal man Adam Kadmon through whom the entire creation is brought into being. Atziluth is the world in which the Tree of Life is first established and through which the divine archetypes are expressed in the lower worlds.

To the world of Briah are attributed the words, 'whom I have *created* for my glory', signifying that this world is where, allegorically speaking, creation is conceived as in the mind of an architect, and wherein the first Adam is created, thus: 'God *created* man in His own image'.[20] This androgynous Adam did not possess a corporeal body, but a body of pure spirit, as yet without form or image. The world of Briah is the throne of Metatron, the Angel of the Presence, and the abode of the holy Archangels.

---

[19] Isaiah 43:7. Italics are mine.

[20] Genesis 1:27.

To the world of Yetzirah are attributed the words, 'I have *formed* him', signifying that this world is where creation is given a form, again allegorically speaking, as in the mind of an artist. It is in this world that the second Adam is formed thus: 'the Lord God *formed* man of the dust of the ground, and breathed into his nostrils the breath of life; and man became a living being'.[21] Adam in this world has both a form and an image, but the substance of his form is of the nature of light. To this world is attributed the choirs of angels, concerning whom Isaac Myer wrote, drawing upon the writings of Ibn Gebirol, 'In this world reside those intelligent and incorporeal beings, each wrapped in a luminous vestment, which are sexless and capable, by the divine permission, of assuming a form sensible to mankind when they appear to him'.[22]

To the world of Assiah are attributed the words, 'Yes, I have *made* him', signifying that this world is where creation takes its most concrete form. It is the world of matter into which Adam fell and was given a coat of skin, thus: 'The Lord God made tunics of skin and clothed them'.[23] In this world Adam and Eve are no longer androgyne but distinctly separate beings, subject to suffering and mortality. This world is under the governance of the planetary and astral forces of the cosmos and is the densest and most concrete of all the worlds. It is a world of contending forces, beneath which lies the abode of evil spirits, which are considered to be the grossest and most deficient of forms. These evil spirits are continually in conflict with the forces of the worlds above, and are particularly injurious to humanity, ever seeking to pervert man's nature and lead it away from following divine law and the path of spiritual regeneration.

From the above we can see that Kabbalistic doctrine demonstrates the existence of four Adams, or one Adam in four modes. These modes are the archetypal, the creative, the formative ,and the world of making. The first cor-

---

21 Genesis 2:7.

22 Isaac Myer, *Qabbalah*, p. 329.

23 Genesis 3:21.

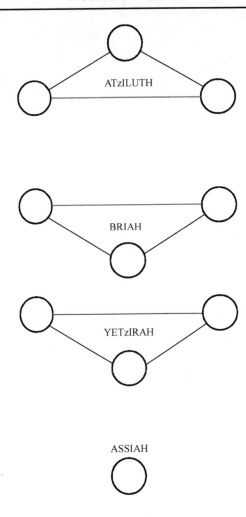

Fig. 14. The four worlds.

responds to Adam Kadmon, the perfect, heavenly archetype of the World of Emanation. The second corresponds
to Adam as a being of pure spirit, a perfect reflection
of Adam Kadmon. The third corresponds to Adam as a
denser and more consolidated simulacrum of the second
Adam. His body is a Body of Light whose natural place
is in the Garden of Eden, or Paradise. The fourth corresponds to the fallen Adam, who is clothed in the body of
flesh. These four modes will repay a great deal of investigation and reflection.

In each of these four worlds reside many kinds of beings,
spiritual and otherwise. In Atziluth, the highest of the
worlds, dwell only the Sephiroth of the archetypal man,
Adam Kadmon. Each Sephira embodies a divine principle
or name. In the second world, the world of Briah, reside the
Archangels under the leadership of Metatron, considered
to be the greatest of the Archangels. The true meaning of
the name Metatron is not known but some sources maintain that his name is derived from *metator*, the Latin for 'a
guide'. He is also identified as the 'Angel of the Presence'
and is charged with the care of humankind. He is said to be
the link between the human and the divine and legend has
it that he incarnated as the patriarch Enoch, although this
claim is contentious. He serves as the scribe in the heavenly court and has been depicted as the masculine form of
the Shekinah, and the angel who led the people of Israel
through the wilderness. He is believed to stand before the
Throne of Glory and also guards the Hekhalot, the seven
halls of light through which the Merkabah mystics (riders
or descenders of the Chariot) must pass in order to reach
the Throne of God.

In the third world, the World of Yetzirah, reside the ten
angelic hosts, presided over by the Archangels. The word
'angel' derives from the Persian *angaros*,[24] meaning a 'courier',

or from the Greek *angelos*, meaning a 'messenger'. They are incorporeal beings, said to be either asexual or androgynous and clothed in garments of light. The angels function as officers of the heavenly realm and must submit to the bidding of the great Archangels. They are set to watch different parts of the universe, over heavenly bodies, people, places, seasons, and times, as well as elemental and cosmic forces. Corresponding with the Malkuth of Yetzirah, the tenth order of angels—the *Ishim*—consists of the beatified souls of just men and women, as described by St. John in Revelation 14: 1–5.

The fourth world, the World of Assiah, the world into which Adam and Eve fell, is the world of matter. It is made up of the grossest elements of the higher worlds, and is the abode of elemental beings. In this world, humanity must struggle with the contending forces that make demands upon the soul. On the one hand there is the call of the spiritual world, inspiring the soul to overcome the instinctive and appetitive nature, and restore itself to its true place in heaven. On the other hand, there are the unceasing and powerful biological drives and needs of this world, forever making their demand. In this world of conflict and suffering, the soul also has to contend with the perverse realms of darkness and demons, for at its lowest level, Assiah is the place of shades and shells. These nether regions are the haunt of evil spirits and demons that feed on them and any other creature they can beguile. Beneath this world is a perverse and inverted world wherein similar creatures reside. This world 'Contains the orders of retrograde spirits corresponding by inversion to the angels of Yetzirah and the arch-fiends corresponding after the same manner to the arch-angels of the Briatic world'.[25] These creatures seek incessantly to undermine and seduce the soul from its true calling. For the Kabbalist there can be no compromise, for such creatures stop at nothing to fulfil their desire to destroy humanity.

---

[24]   Gustav Davidson, *A Dictionary of Angels* (New York: Collier-Macmillan Ltd., 1967), p. 20.

[25]   Waite, *The Holy Kabbalah*, p. 256.

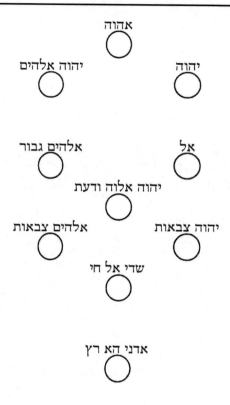

1. EHEIEH   אהוה
2. JEHOVAH   יהוה
3. JEHOVAH ELOHIM   יהוה אלהים
4. EL   אל
5. ELOHIM GIBOR   אלהים נבור
6. JEHOVAH ELOAH VADAATh   יהוה אלוה ודעת
7. JEHOVAH TzABAOTh   יהוה צבאות
8. ELOHIM TzABAOTh   אלהים צבאות
9. SHADDAI EL ChAI   שרי אל חי
10. ADONAI HA ARETz   אדני הא רץ

Fig. 15. Atziluth and the divine names of God.

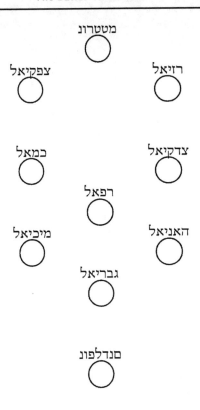

1. METATRON   מטטרון
2. RAZIEL   רזיאל
3. TzPhQIEL   צפקיאל
4. TzDQIEL   צדקיאל
5. KMEL   כמאל
6. RPhEL   רפאל
7. HANIEL   האניאל
8. MIKEL   מיכיאל
9. GBRIEL   גבריאל
10. SNDLPhVN   סנדלפון

Fig. 16. Briah and the ten archangels.

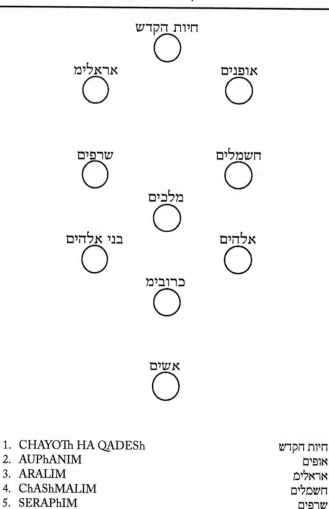

1. CHAYOTh HA QADESh   חיות הקדש
2. AUPhANIM   אופים
3. ARALIM   אראלימ
4. ChAShMALIM   חשמלים
5. SERAPhIM   שרפים
6. MALAKHIM   מלכים
7. ELOHIM   אלהים
8. BENI ELOHIM   בני אלהים
9. KERUBIM   כרובים
10. ISHIM   אשים

Fig. 17. Yetzirah and the ten orders of angels.

1.	RAShIThHA GLGLIM	(*Primum Mobile*)	ראשית הא גלגלים
2.	MZLVTh	(*Sphere of the Zodiac*)	מזלות
3.	ShBThAI	(*Sphere of Saturn*)	שבתאי
4.	TzDQ	(*Sphere of Jupiter*)	צדק
5.	MDIM	(*Sphere of Mars*)	מדים
6.	ShMSh	(*Sphere of the Sun*)	שמש
7.	NVGH	(*Sphere of Venus*)	נוגה
8.	KVKB	(*Sphere of Mercury*)	כוכב
9.	LBNH	(*Sphere of the Moon*)	לבנת
10.	OVLM ISVDVTh	(*Sphere of Elements*)	עולם יסודות

Fig. 18. Assiah and the ten houses, or heavens.

THE TETRAGRAMMATON

The word 'tetragrammaton' derives from the Greek, *tetra,* meaning 'four', and *gramma,* meaning 'letter'. It is a word with four letters; therefore, any four-letter word constitutes a tetragrammaton. However, the Tetragrammaton referred to here is a term that was used by early Kabbalists to denote the unutterable name of God. In ancient Israel, among the Hebrews, the speaking of this name—יהוה, IHVH, Jehovah (or Jahweh)—was forbidden, except to the high priest, and then only once a year in the Temple, on the Day of Atonement. Otherwise it was considered blasphemous for anyone to utter the name aloud, the punishment for which was death. A pious Jew, encountering the word when reading the scriptures aloud, replaces YHVH with the word ADNI— *Adonai*—which means 'lord', or uses the name *Elohim* in places where repetition is likely to occur. According to Kabbalistic doctrine it is taught that the true pronunciation of the Great Name YHVH has been lost to mankind. Some say it was lost at the time of the Babylonian destruction of the first Temple, others say it was lost at the time of the destruction of the second Temple, when the armies of Rome destroyed the Kingdom of Israel. Others claim it was lost at the passing of Simeon ben Yohai, the great second-century sage and reputed author of the Zohar. Whatever the truth of the matter may be, the Tetragrammaton lies at the very heart of Kabbalah and much of the secret doctrine is concerned with it.

The word itself may seem a straightforward thing to enunciate from an English language perspective, but this is not the case with Semitic languages, which do not have true vowels, but have instead vowel points or marks that indicate how the word might be pronounced. This in itself is no simple matter as originally Hebrew was written without vowel

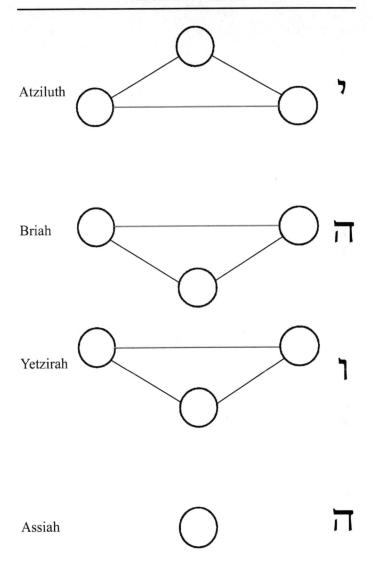

Fig. 19. The Tetragrammaton in four worlds on the Tree.

points, and the vocalization of words was something that was passed on by word of mouth. This only began to change during the Talmudic period (between the second and sixth centuries A.D.) when punctuation systems began to emerge.

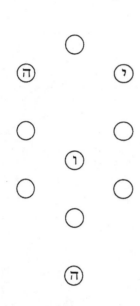

A detailed explanation of this complex subject is beyond the reach of this work, but the interested reader may refer to an informative article, 'Pronunciations of Hebrew' in the *Encyclopedia Judaica*.[26]

Whatever the truth might be concerning the nature and timing of this loss, the fact remains that for a very long time Kabbalists have been left to work with the consonants YHVH, which are pronounced, as it were, symbolically. This has never been an issue to the faithful of the Jewish religion, who do not seek to utter the name out of the context of the law. However,

Fig. 20. The Tetragrammaton on the Tree of Life.

it has been for centuries the focal point, if not the obsession, of countless magicians and other esoterically minded people. Indeed, magicians and wonder-workers have included it in magical formulas from the earliest times and it is to be found in numerous medieval magical texts and grimoires. Whether such formulas are efficacious or not—and many would stand in defence of both sides of the argument—the Tetragrammaton has ever been considered sacred, and even when used symbolically is immensely powerful, particularly to those whose minds are open aright. Yet, it must be said

---

26 Volume 13, p. 1119.

that in many ways the sanctity and efficacy of this name resides not merely in its utterance, but also in the cipher of the written word. As such it is a key to the esoteric doctrines of the Kabbalah, for the reality is that to the Kabbalist the name is the all-encompassing name of God containing the entire creation in its primal expression. Thus it is written in the Sepher Yetzirah that God, 'By the power of His Name made every creature and everything that is; and the production of all things from the twenty-two letters is the proof that they are all but parts of one living body'.[27]

This living body is the Tetragrammaton, the letters of which represent and enclose all ten of the Sephiroth. There are several ways of viewing this. One way is to consider the four worlds as an extension of the Tetragrammaton as illustrated on the preceding page. In another approach the uppermost tip of the ' (Yod) represents Kether, while the bulk of its body represents Chokmah; the first ה (Hé) represents Binah and the ו (Vau) represents Tiphereth and the five Sephiroth surrounding it. The final ה represents Malkuth. In practise the ' (Yod) defines the masculine principle of Chokmah, it is the Supernal Father. *Heh* ה defines the feminine principle of Binah, it is the Supernal Mother. The union of Yod and Hé generates the entire

Fig. 21. The body of the Tetragrammaton.

creation, and everything that exists within it. Creation is represented by ו (Vau), the son, who is a reflection, as it were, of Yod, the Supernal Father. His place is Tiphereth and the

27 Westcott, *Sepher Yetzirah*, p. 19.

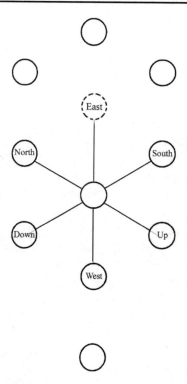

Fig. 22. The six directions on the Tree of Life.

five Sephiroth that surround it. The final Hé is a reflection of the Supernal Mother; her place is Malkuth, which is naturally receptive and feminine, receiving and giving form to the potencies of all the Sephiroth preceding it. Although she is sometimes called the 'Daughter of the Seven', she is more fittingly known as the 'Bride of Macroprosopus' (Tiphereth), and through their union the world is sustained.

The Tetragrammaton can also be viewed as the body of a man (figure 21, p. 27), where the ' represents the head, the ה represents the shoulders and arms, the ו represents the torso, and the final ה represents the hips and legs. The same arrangement may be contemplated as a symbol of the divine archetype, or it may be viewed as a cipher of the spiritual matrix of the soul in a form of a man arranged upon the tree, which in itself is extremely suggestive. However it is viewed the Tetragrammaton forms an icon worthy of prolonged meditation.

Another way of viewing the Tetragrammaton as a cipher is based upon the following text:

> He selected three letters from among the simple ones and sealed them and formed them into a Great Name, IHV, and with this He sealed the Universe in six directions. He looked above, and sealed the Height with IHV. He looked below and sealed the Depth with IVH. He looked forward, and sealed the East with HIV. He looked backward, and sealed the West with HVI. He looked to the right, and sealed the South with VIH. He looked to the left, and sealed the North with VHI. Behold! From the Ten ineffable Sephiroth do proceed—the One Spirit of the Gods of the living, Air, Water, Fire; and also Height, Depth, East, West, South and North.[28]

Here is a formula, written in a symbolic language that defines the parameters of the three-dimensional world in which we have our existence. Above, below, before, behind, left, and right, these terms define how we experience our world, and both our biological and psychological functions are dependent upon them. This need not be taken only literally; for we are dealing with a symbolic language that describes how the infinite and therefore unknowable nature of the godhead is expressed in creation through the Sephiroth—the sublime vehicles of divine potential manifest in the form of Adam Kadmon. YHVH, then, is a cipher representing the presence of the divine En-Sof in creation, and when understood

---

28 Westcott, *Sepher Yetzirah*, p. 17.

correctly, establishes a sacred space in which we are established and sanctified by the name and presence of God—the Tetragrammaton.

Another name by which the Tetragrammaton is known is 'the Ineffable Name' or *Shemhamaphoresh*. This 72-syllable name of God is based upon a very ancient formula constructed from verses 19, 20, and 21 of Exodus, chapter 14. Each of these verses contains seventy-two letters; and seventy-two syllables are formed by combining them in a particular way. These names were often used to form talismans.[29] The connection between the Tetragrammaton and the Shemhamaphoresh may be seen by arranging the cipher of IHVH in the form of a Pythagorean *tetractys*; an interesting gematric equation unfolds (see figure 22 below).

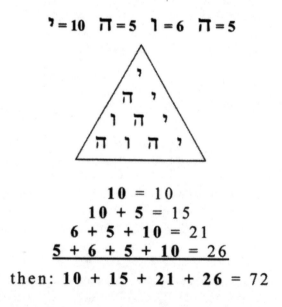

Fig. 23. The Tetragrammaton as Pythagorean tetractys.

29 *Ibid.*, p. 28.

Chapter 3

Language and Number

HEBREW WAS THE language of the Jewish people in biblical times. Originally it was based upon an archaic alphabet known as the Proto-Canaanite Script, which arose during the second millennium B.C., and was probably inspired by Egyptian hieroglyphics. However, toward the end of this period a unique Hebrew alphabet emerged derived from the script developed by the people of Phoenicia (now Lebanon). It was an alphabet based on sounds rather than signs and symbols, and many other alphabets were subsequently derived from it, including Aramaic and archaic Greek.

Hebrew was widely used in the ancient kingdom of Israel until the country was overrun first by the Assyrians in the eighth century B.C. and then by the Babylonians in the sixth century B.C., following which the Hebrew script was gradually displaced by Aramaic, and had almost totally disappeared by the first century; the Jews of first century Palestine spoke Aramaic, not Hebrew. Aramaic originated in the region we now know as Syria; and probably as a consequence of the success of the Assyrian empire (ninth–seventh centuries B.C.) it became established as an international language, written and

spoken throughout the Levant, Mesopotamia, Egypt, and
Persia. It was readily adopted in Israel, superseding Hebrew,
which remained in use only in religious rites and ceremonies
until the formation of the new state of Israel in the mid-twentieth century. When the Jews adopted the Aramaic writing,
they evolved from it a script called Square Hebrew, which is
how most people would recognise it today.

The Hebrew alphabet has 22 letters, all consonants. Symbols or marks for the vowels were introduced around the
eighth century A.D. and are usually placed below the consonants. Hebrew is written from right to left. Each letter has a
specific sound, name, number, symbol, and quality, suggesting different levels of understanding.

CONCERNING THE ALPHABET AND NUMBER

To the Kabbalist the letters of the Hebrew alphabet are more
than simple components of words; the correspondences of
each letter are very extensive. Not only does every letter have
a sound but it also has a name, a numerical value, and a form,
all of which play a significant part in Kabbalah. Furthermore
each letter has an associated image and an astrological symbol. For example, the letter Aleph א has the value of 1, or,
when written larger, the value of 1,000. It may also be viewed
as an ox or interpreted as the element of air. The shape of the
letter itself is said to describe a bull, and in some circles it is
said to represent a man standing with his arms outstretched.
At a high level, Aleph symbolises the One, the eternal and
omnipotent God. It is the principal channel between heaven
and earth, and when considered as such it describes a flow
of life between one and the other, thus some Kabbalists have
likened it to Jacob's ladder.[1]

---

[1]   Jacob's ladder: As he slept one night with his head upon a stone, Jacob
saw, in his dream, the angels ascending and descending a ladder from earth
to heaven (Gen. 28:12).

The Kabbalist accepts as a matter of fact that the scriptures were given to us by divine inspiration, that they are the Word of God, the divine will made manifest in our world. Thus, the analysis of the sacred texts is taken very seriously; indeed, every sentence, every word, and every letter is counted, compared, and reflected upon. Because numbers also represents the letters, it is possible to establish the numerical value of any word or phrase. On this basis several systems of working with the letters have been established. These systems are ancient, and have proved to be invaluable tools for exploring the hidden depths of scripture.

This may seem strange, even obsessive, to the majority of people who think of numbers as simply being tools for establishing quantity and value. Today, significant meaning in number rarely goes beyond dates of birthdays, anniversaries, and lucky numbers, but in the ancient world number had a profound, if not sacred, import that would have been lost to humanity if it had not been preserved in various societies of devoted scholars and quiet sanctuaries of esoteric schools. In our rational, secularised world, the mystical and symbolic interpretation of number is either associated with historical figures such as Pythagoras and his successors or with periods of social decadence such as that of the Greco-Roman world of late antiquity. In our time, such interests are considered to be delusory and generally associated with the eccentrics who populate the fringes of our society.

However, it is a fact that throughout the ancient world the mystical significance of number was at least as important as its scientific application. But times have changed, and the mind of humanity is now focussed upon an exploration of the material world and the development of a material philosophy and science that excludes all that lies outside its perceived area of interest; including religion and all things connected with the life of the soul. This was probably inevitable;

Table 3. Basic correspondences.

Name	Hebrew	English	Numeric Value	Astro-logical Symbol	Sound	Image
Aleph	א	A	1	Aerus	Mother	Ox
Beth	ב	B	2	☿	Double	House
Gimel	ג	G	3	☽	Double	Camel
Daleth	ד	D	4	♀	Double	Door
Heh	ה	H	5	♈	Simple	Window
Vau	ו	V	6	♉	Simple	Peg/Nail
Zain	ז	Z	7	♊	Simple	Sword
Cheth	ח	Ch	8	♋	Simple	Enclosure
Teth	ט	T	9	♌	Simple	Serpent
Yod	י	I	10	♍	Simple	Hand
Kaph	כ	K	20	♃	Double	Palm of hand
Lamed	ל	L	30	♎	Simple	Ox goad
Mem	מ	M	40	Aqua	Mother	Water
Nun	נ	N	50	♏	Simple	Fish
Samech	ס	S	60	♐	Simple	Prop/support
Ayin	ע	O	70	♑	Simple	Eye
Phe	פ	P	80	♂	Double	Mouth
Tzaddi	צ	Tz	90	♒	Simple	Fish hook
Qoph	ק	Q	100	♓	Simple	Back of head
Resh	ר	R	200	☉	Double	Head
Shin	ש	Sh	300	Ignis	Mother	Tooth
Tau	ת	Th	400	♄	Double	Sign of Cross

nevertheless the appreciation of the role that number plays in the spiritual dimension of human life has continued unabated from classical times, albeit in reduced circumstances, and nowhere has it been more appreciated than in the esoteric schools of Diaspora Judaism that were eventually to give rise to the Kabbalists of the medieval era and beyond.

The spirit of scriptural interpretation, aided by a metaphysical understanding of the meaning of number, has ever been an important feature of the Kabbalah, and without an appreciation of this fact those who seek to engage in the work of Kabbalah will find themselves struggling to understand the different systems employed therein. The following notes about some of the key features of the classical world's perception of the meaning and philosophy of the basic numbers one to ten may thus be of value.

Number One

One emerges out of the monad, which is the term used to express the principle of Unity. The monad was understood by Pythagorean and Platonic philosophers to signify the first cause of creation, out of which emerge all things, including the number one, which in a paradoxical way is synonymous with the monad but distinct from it. In nature it is the potential for diversity demonstrated in geometry by a point and in mathematics by the number one. As such it is the cause, source, beginning, and basis of all number and numeration. They also understood that all even numbers were feminine and that all odd numbers were masculine, except for the monad, which is absolutely androgynous, because it is the father and mother of all number.

Number Two

Two indicates division and polarization. It is the first step from unity into diversity. The emergence of duality and diversification out of unity points to a polarization of the number one and in doing so gives rise to contraries that can be expressed numerically. The number two signifies matter. In the Pythagorean tradition there are three stages of creation, the first is unity symbolised by the monad, the second is polarization into two opposite creative powers, symbolised by the duad, the third is the uniting of these opposites in the generation of life, symbolised by the triad.

Number Three

If we accept the number one as a point, and the number two as a line, then the number three corresponds to the plane. The smallest plane imaginable is the triangle, which is the basis of the first three-dimensional figure—the three-sided pyramid. The number three causes the potential of the monad to advance into actuality and extension and is therefore considered the basis of Creation. It reconciles the polarities engendered through the actions of the number two; thus it has been called the number of friendship, harmony, peace, and unanimity. It indicates a beginning, a middle, and an end, and also implies a past, a present, and a future. Thus it speaks of form and time, of experience and knowledge. Out of these is born the world of duality, or in modern terms, 'space-time'.

Number Four

The number four is considered to be the begetter of the decad because the sum of all the numbers contained within it totals ten (1 + 2 + 3 + 4). It is known as the 'foundation', because in geometrical procession it is the first number to display the nature of three-dimensional existence: point, line, plane, solid. Its forms are considered to be the tetrahedron pyramid (the first solid), because it consists of four angles and four planes, and the cube, because it is a three-dimensional square—the symbol of earth. The tetrad gives rise to the four elements and universal existence, and as such signifies the quality and nature of change. It is understood that the monad applies to arithmetic, the dyad to music, the triad to geometry, and the tetrad to astronomy.

Number Five

Five is thought to be androgynous, consisting as it does of the first masculine and feminine numbers (two and three) and because it was formed of male and female it was called 'marriage'. It was also understood to consist of the four elements plus æther (spirit) and was therefore called 'lack of strife', because through the fifth element of spirit it reconciles any potential discordance. The pentad also signifies justice, because it governs equality in the soul and regulates providence, again through the element of æther.

Number Six

Six is thought to be the first perfect number because it arises out of the multiplication of the first even and odd numbers; it was also thought to be androgynous and to signify marriage because of the relationship between these two numbers (two and three). Because it was understood to be the form of forms, possessing wholeness, it was accepted as a symbol of the soul, and that the universe was ensouled and harmonised by it, and through it attained wholeness, permanence, health, and beauty. It signifies the six directions of extensions of solid bodies: up, down, forward, backward, left, and right.

Number Seven

Seven is believed to be a virgin born neither of mother (even number) or father (odd number) but from the father of all (the monad). It was revered by the ancient philosophers, and called 'that which brings to completion'. It was understood that all things, both in the heavens and upon the earth, were brought to completion by it, thus because it controlled mortal affairs it was called 'chance'. The soul is understood to descend into existence through the seven planetary spheres, acquiring its qualities or virtues from them. It also applied to the seven liberal arts and sciences, which were devised for the edification of the soul.

Number Eight

Eight was known to the ancient Platonic and Pythagorean philosophers as 'perfect harmony'. The eighth sphere of the heavens—which was understood to contain the zodiac—encompassed all of the planetary regions, and as such has a particular significance concerning the harmony of the spheres, thus the number eight was considered to be the source of all musical ratios. Philolaus, a Pythagorean philosopher of the fifth century B.C., is attributed with the saying:

> . . . that after mathematical magnitude has become three-dimensional, thanks to the tetrad, there is quality and 'colour' of visible nature in the pentad, and ensoulment in the hexad, and intelligence and health and what he calls 'light' in the Hebdomad, and then next, with the Ogdoad, things come by love and friendship and wisdom and creative thought.[2]

---

[2] Iamblichus, *The Theology of Arithmetic: On the Mystical, Mathematical and Cosmological Symbolism of the First Ten Numbers*, Robin Waterfield, trans. (Grand Rapids, MI: Phanes Press, 1988), p. 103.

Number Nine

Nine is considered to be the greatest of all numbers within the decad. It was also called 'the perfector', '. . . because it gives completion to the fabrication of generation' (Proclus). As the end of a sequence of numbers, it signifies the end of the formation of specific identities; for number admits nothing beyond the Ennead, returning as it does to the monad in the decad.

Number Ten

The number ten, the decad, is understood to signify the universe because it is the most perfect boundary of number. It denotes the completion of building, bringing everything to fulfilment. It was called 'eternity' because it contains all things in itself. Thus it was recognised by the philosophers of the ancient world that there were ten heavenly spheres in which creation is contained. The decad was venerated by the Pythagoreans as the tetraktys, a triangular representation of the combination of the first four numbers $(1 + 2 + 3 + 4)$. It was also called 'fate' because all numbers, things and events were sown into it.

This brief overview is far from exhaustive, but it will, perhaps, have demonstrated in some small way the reverence the philosophers of the ancient world had for the mystical significance of number, a reverence that was undoubtedly shared to some degree by many people of the day. Of course, it is probably true that much of society was then, as it is today, given over to common superstitions and vulgar practises, which at the collective level debase the profound spirituality and metaphysics underpinning the mystical appreciation of number. But, in the Kabbalistic schools this ancient knowledge was firmly tied to the spiritual exploration and understanding of the Torah;

there never was room for idle speculation. Consequently in Kabbalah number has evolved into a powerful tool that opens up surprising dimensions in the understanding of the language of the scriptures and of certain ideas communicated therein. The Torah is the 'Law', and it is expected that all true disciples should study the Law, to understand it as best they can. However, the written Torah is but a garment concealing a deeper meaning; this deeper meaning is known as the 'Soul of the Law', and it is to the Soul of the Law that the Kabbalist goes in search of understanding. It is an interior journey wherein the soul reflects upon the significance of the scriptures. To do this effectively the soul must direct and control the unruly will. Left to its own devices the will, except in extremely rare cases, generally gravitates to the comfort zone of old behaviour patterns. In simple terms, the attention wanders, and it must be brought back to the main objective which is the study of the scriptures, wherein it may learn the way of the divine and may grow in understanding. Such work is known as meditation, and some of the most useful tools used by the Kabbalists in meditation involve the symbolism of numbers and their correspondences.

THE THIRTY-TWO PATHS OF WISDOM

> In thirty-two mysterious Paths of Wisdom did Jah, the Jehovah of hosts, the God of Israel, the Living Elohim, the King of ages, the merciful and gracious God the Exalted One, the Dweller in eternity, most high and holy—engrave his name by the three Sepharim— Numbers, Letters and Sounds.

These words are the opening lines of the Sepher Yetzirah, concerning which a great deal of marvellous speculation has been written, and no doubt will continue to be written in the future. Much of the speculation is of a very learned nature and requires prolonged study before it begins to make sense. This does not mean that the Kabbalah is only for scholars, far from it: but there are a number of factors that do need to be taken into account by anyone seeking a greater understanding of this subject. One of these factors is that the language of the Kabbalah is a language of metaphor and allegory, employed to conceal a sacred teaching from the curious, but designed to be understood by those who have been given the keys.

Consider then, the first line, which states, 'In thirty-two mysterious paths of Wisdom'. These words are pregnant with meaning. For example, in Hebrew the number 32 is written לב, which is the Hebrew word for the heart. Now there is a teaching concerning the heart that has been fundamental to the tradition since time immemorial. It is a teaching concerned with concentrating the mind in the region of the heart, as opposed to the brain and the physical senses. The heart is in fact the 'Inner Temple', the entrance to which is only revealed to those whose conscience has been purified; thus, to enter the Inner Temple one must first learn the method of purifying the conscience—and there is a method. Those who are fortunate enough to discover this method may then enter the temple of the heart. However, the method is not easy to implement and requires a great deal of patience and fortitude. In part this is because consciousness is essentially modal, and the mode in which we normally experience life is reactive and transient, ever dependent upon data from the senses and body chemistry to define reality, and thus incapable of grasping the profound realities of the Sephirotic world, which is the constant unchanging substrate of our existence.

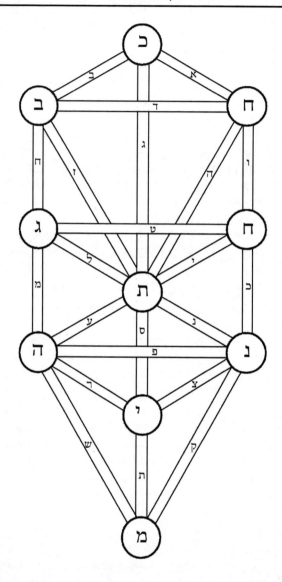

Fig. 24. The thirty-two paths of wisdom.

Simply put, this means we must withdraw the mind from the material world of the senses and concentrate it within the heart. This is a very particular discipline involving a slow and systematic withdrawal from the external senses and from the attachments we have formed to the things of the senses. It is not simply a question of technique, or words of power, but requires a love of the divine that is greater and more persistent than our love of the world or self. Different schools have their own methods designed to bring this about, which when successfully applied result in the mind being established in the heart and functioning in an altogether more exalted mode of consciousness. 'Wisdom' is a title of the second Sephirah, Chokmah. It describes a state of unity that transcends duality and that is, strictly speaking, beyond the grasp of human consciousness. Nevertheless, its influence is experienced in the heart as a state of being in which the soul is embraced in the peace and love of God. It is in this blessed state that the soul is able to engage with the Sephirotic world, and in which the mysteries of creation are revealed according to thirty-two mysterious (or secret) paths.

These paths are described in the Sepher Yetzirah and are represented therein by the ten Sephiroth and the twenty-two letters of the Hebrew alphabet (see figure 24, p. 80). The Sephiroth, which constitute the body of the divine Adam Kadmon, are described as the first ten paths. The twenty-two letters, which convention describes as the interconnecting paths between the Sephiroth, constitute a sophisticated metaphysical language that describes the chemistry of creation. As letters they may be contemplated in three different ways; as the written word, as the spoken word, and as number. In all three ways there are mysteries and secrets. They are also attributed, according to an ancient cosmology, to three primary elements, seven planets, and twelve signs of the zodiac; upon which an archaic, and some would say universal, mystical teaching

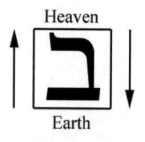

Fig. 25. The letter and manifestation.

depends. According to the Sepher Yetzirah the letters are derived from the Sephiroth, thus: 'The ineffable Sephiroth give forth the ten numbers. First; the Spirit of the God of the living; second; from the Spirit He produced Air, and formed in it twenty-two sounds— the letters'.[3] The formation of each letter is based upon a square: the top represents the heavens; the right-hand side is a descending line from heaven; the bottom represents the earth; and the left-hand side is an ascending line, suggesting a movement into and out of manifestation (see figure 25).

LETTERS AND NUMBERS AS MEDITATION TOOLS

In this section are described some of the more important methods used by Kabbalists in their meditations and philosophical speculations. These methods involve the permutations of letters and number according to definite rules of engagement. They enable Kabbalists to engage in a profound exploration of the scriptures; to penetrate beyond the literal meaning of the sacred texts, bringing them, it is taught, to the inner sanctuary of the soul, where the spirit of God descends and assists them in the work of spiritual regeneration and prepares them for the work of assisting their fellows. These methods are ancient, indeed, their use was well understood by the ancient priests and scribes of Egypt, Babylon, and Persia, and were later to become widespread in the Hellenistic world.

---

[3] Westcott, *Sepher Yetzirah*, p. 16.

Gematria

This is a method of scriptural exegesis through which the numerical value of words or phrases is calculated and used to establish a more esoteric understanding of the text. The comparison with other words and phrases of a similar value is an added dimension to this method, and has been used extensively by Kabbalists from the earliest times. The first recorded use of Gematria occurs in an inscription of the Babylonian king, Sargon II,[4] which states that he built the wall of Khorsabad 16,283 cubits long to correspond with the numerical value of his name. Its use was widespread in the Hellenistic world, and it is known to have been used by the teachers of the Mishna in Palestine during the second century and by the medieval Kabbalists from the twelfth century onward. One example, from Genesis 18:2, is as follows: 'Lo! Three men stood by him'.[5] It is deduced that these three men were in fact the angels Michael, Gabriel, and Raphael, because the numerical values of והנה שלשה (*and lo! Three men*) and אל ומיכאל נבריכאל ורפאל (*These are Michael, Gabriel, and Raphael*) are the same (see figure 26).

ה	ש	ל	ש	ה	נ	ה	ו
5	300	30	300	5	50	5	6
ל	א	כ	י	מ	ו	ל	א
30	1	20	10	40	6	30	1
ל	א	י	ר	ב	נ		
30	1	10	200	2	3		
ל	א	פ	ר	ו			
30	1	80	200	6			

Fig. 26. An example of gematria.

---

4 727–707 B.C.

5 *Septuagint.*

Notarikon

Notarikon is a system of shorthand in which the letters of a word are seen as an abbreviation of a whole sentence, or conversely, where the initial letters of each word in a sentence are combined to form a word that could be used to throw light on the original sentence. The term is derived from the system used by a shorthand writer in the law courts of ancient Rome. These *Notarii*, as they were called, were skilled at abbreviating sentences and frequently signified whole words by single letters. For example, the word AGLA אגלא is composed of the first letters of (read right to left):

$$\text{אדני לעולם גבור ה את}$$

and which means in English, 'Thou art mighty forever my Lord'. The word 'amen', is said to be composed from the initials of אדני מלך נאמן, which reads in English 'The Lord and faithful King'. Another example is based upon the first word of the Bible, בראשית, *Bereshith*, which forms:

$$\text{תורה ישראל שיקבלו אליהים את ראשית בראשית}$$

meaning, 'In the beginning God saw that Israel would accept the Law'. There are other variations of this method, including joining the beginnings and endings of words together and or connecting two words in the same sentence to make one. These methods were central to the meditative techniques devised in the 13th century by Abraham Abulafia, and were used extensively in his school and by those who succeeded him. He used the techniques for developing the power of association, through which the attention of the aspirant progresses in an undistracted stream of connected thought wherein may be revealed profound spiritual truths. His methods were further developed by his successors.

Temurah

Temurah is a method of substituting letters according to specific rules; sometimes the letters of a word or phrase are transposed as shown in Table 4.

Table 4. Hebrew letters and transposition.

1	2	3	4	5	6	7	8	9	10	20
א	ב	ג	ד	ה	ו	ז	ח	ט	י	כ
ת	ש	ר	ק	צ	פ	ע	ס	נ	מ	ל
400	300	200	100	90	80	70	60	50	40	30

Aleph א then becomes the letter Tau ת, and Beth ב becomes the letter Shin ש, and so on. There are another twenty-one variations of this particular system, a system known in some circles as the 'Combination of Tziruph'. Alternatively, each letter of a word is replaced by another according to a given scheme, thereby forming a new word. There are countless permutations of this nature, few of which are concerned with the esoteric understanding of Scripture. One of the most common is known as *AiQ Bekar*, or the 'Kabbalah of Nine Chambers'. This is produced by intersecting two horizontal lines with two vertical lines, forming something like the board for noughts and crosses, as shown in figure 27.

נלש	בכר	איק
וסם	הנך	דמת
טצץ	חפף	זען

Fig. 27. AiQ Bekar, the Kabbalah of Nine Chambers.

The letters are arranged in each square according to their values in units tens and hundreds, thus Aleph א = 1, Yod י = 10 and Qoph ק = 100; Beth ב = 2, Kaph כ = 20, Resh ר = 200. Many other systems based on Temurah, were developed during and after the late medieval period, and are more suited to the occult and political machinations of 17th and 18th-century Europe than in understanding the spiritual dimensions of Kabbalah.[6]

THE MAGICAL USE OF THE LETTERS

The disciplines discussed so far have little to do with magic. Undoubtedly there are magical aspects to Kabbalah, but in the main, outside of the schools, these disciplines have been distorted through greed, ignorance, and a lack of understanding. Generally speaking, the magical dynamics of Practical Kabbalah are based upon the 'transformative' nature and power of the sacred names of God and the hierarchy of angels that exist in the spiritual worlds, and it has long been recognised by Kabbalists that through engaging with these powerful agencies it is possible to effect changes not only in these spiritual worlds but in the physical world as well. However, it would be negligent of me if I did not point out that what is commonly associated with Kabbalah as magic has in fact little to do with Kabbalah, or with its primary objectives, which are generally concerned with the regeneration of the soul rather than with wonder-working or astral tourism.

The majority of true Kabbalists openly disavow many of the magical practises commonly associated with Practical Kabbalah, as they are not only irrelevant to the regeneration of the soul but they often embrace dangerous practises that inevitably disrupt the natural order of things, and frequently forge unlawful connections between forces and entities that should be kept

---

[6]   An interesting discussion of this subject is to be found in Ruth Tatlow's book, *Bach and the Riddle of the Number Alphabet* (Cambridge, England: Cambridge University Press, 1991).

separate. Such activities are considered to be a rebellion against the will of God as established in the natural laws of creation. Much of what passes in the world today as magic is more an invention of recent times than of the ancient world. This also applies to Kabbalah. Many connections have been attributed to ancient Kabbalists and their schools in support of the credentials of questionable systems of magic and general occult practises. A great deal of these practises are concerned with different forms of psychism—the development of psychic faculties that enable entities, spiritual or otherwise, to use one's mind as a vehicle for various enterprises that may be deemed vital to the well-being of the individual, or even for humanity. It should be noted that this field of endeavour is full of pitfalls and dangers.

In *The Book of Talismans* the authors state:

> THE KABALA, the source and inspiration of the numerous talismans, came into being very soon after the establishment of the Christian Religion, when the Jewish Rabbis developed a complete science of Divine things, received, as the name implies, by direct revelation, according to which all created things from the highest to the lowest are ruled, through the ten principal names of God, acting first through the nine orders of the Angelic Hosts and blessed souls, and through them to the Celestial Spheres, Planets, and Mankind. Lower degrees of Angels and celestial influences, known as Intelligences, rule each element, nation, language, animal and vegetable life, atmospheric conditions, emotions and aspirations. The early Christians had great faith and belief in the power of numbers, and their magical formulas were largely composed of letters having numerical values, usually expressed in Hebrew. Sometimes Greek letters were used, which, when combined with astrological formulas, attracted the good influences of the Angels and Intelligences ruling through the Planets, the houses of the Zodiac, their triplicities and degrees'.[7]

---

[7]   William and Kate Pavitt, *The Book of Talismans* (London: Bracken Books, 1993), pp. 114–115.

They were probably alluding to the Sepher Yetzirah, which from the earliest times Kabbalists have claimed was composed by the patriarch Abraham, and passed on orally from generation to generation, being written down, and then only in cryptic form, at a much later date, probably in the time of the Exile. However, today it is generally accepted that it was put into a written format some time in the late second or early third century A.D. It is a short text that describes thirty-two paths of wisdom, ten of which correspond to the Sephiroth and twenty-two to the letters of the Hebrew alphabet. For more than fifteen hundred years this enigmatic text has influenced leading figures in esoteric communities throughout the Western world. It describes an ancient cosmology, the essence of which is contained in the following extract. The twenty-two letters are allocated to the primary elements, the signs of the zodiac, and the planets; three of the letters are attributed to the primary elements of air, fire and water; seven are attributed to the seven planets of the ancient cosmological arrangement; finally twelve are attributed to the twelve signs of the zodiac. Its influence upon esoteric circles cannot be overestimated, even today:

> The Lord of Hosts, the Living God, King of the Universe, omnipotent, All kind and merciful, supreme and extolled, Who is eternal, sublime and Most-Holy, ordained (formed) and created the Universe in thirty-two mysterious paths of wisdom by three Seraphim, namely; i) S'for; ii) Sipper; and iii) Sapher, which are for Him one and the same.
>
> They consist of a decade out of nothing, and of twenty-two fundamental letters. He divided the twenty-two consonants into three divisions; 1) Three Mothers, fundamental letters or first elements. 2) seven double; and 3) twelve simple consonants.[8]

---

[8]   Isidor Kalisch, *The Sepher Yezirah* (Gillette, New Jersey: Heptangle Books, 1987) p. 3.

Concerning this, William Wynn Westcott writes:

> From this origin arose a system of designing talismans written on parchment or engraved on brass or gems: as each planet has a letter and a number, in regard to each a Magic Square of lesser squares; thus for Jupiter 4 was the number and Daleth ד the letter, and the Magic Square of Jupiter had 16 smaller squares within it; in each a number 1 to 16, and so each line added up to 34 and the total of numbers was 136. Every talisman duly formed bore at least one God name to sanctify it: notable names were IH, Jah; ALH, Eloah; then IHVH; then the notable 42 lettered name, which was really composed of others— Aheie asher aheie (I am that I am) Jah, Jehuiah, Al, Elohim, Jehovah, Tzabaoth, Al Chai and Adonai.[9]

Table 5. Astrological attributions of the Hebrew alphabet.

9 W. W. Westcott, *The Kabbalah* (London: John Watkins, 1926), pp. 27–28.

ד	יד	יה	א
ט	ז	ו	יב
ה	יא	י	ח
יו	ב	ג	יג

4	14	15	1
9	7	6	12
5	11	10	8
16	2	3	13

Fig. 28. The Magic Square of Jupiter.

Another application of the letter to talismans is the seventy-two names of God known as the Shemhamphorash or 'separated name'. There are different views about the origin of this name. Some believe it was composed in medieval Europe, while others claim it has existed from ancient times. It was certainly well-known to the authors of the Bahir and the Zohar, and was used extensively by Abulafia and his school in the latter half of the 13th century. If it was known in ancient times the method of composing and using it was not common knowledge, even among Kabbalists, until Abulafia made it available.

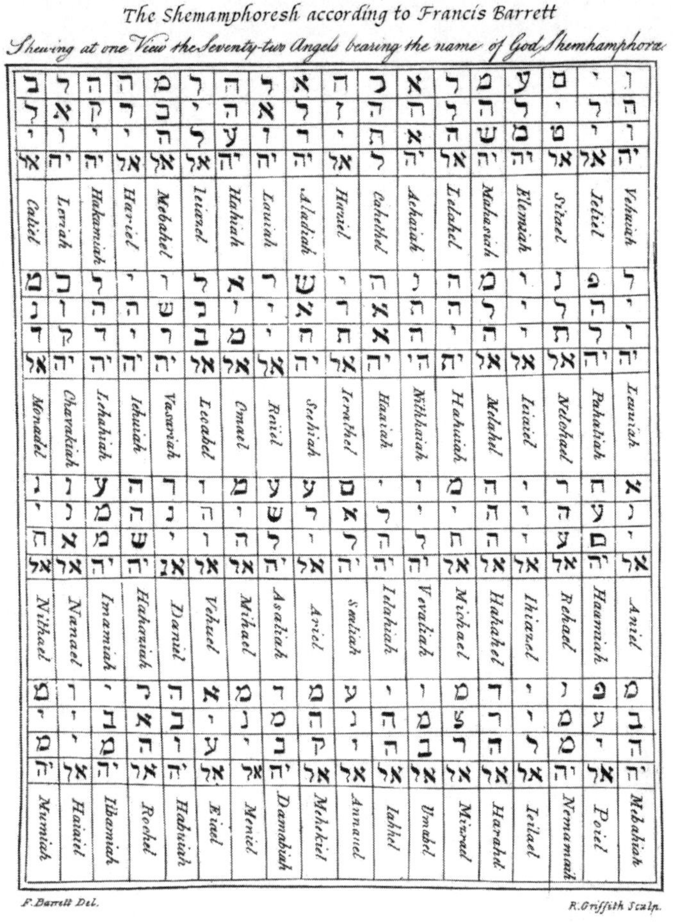
The Shemamphoresh according to Francis Barrett
Shewing at one View the Seventy-two Angels bearing the name of God Shemhamphora
Vehuiah
Jeliel
Sitael
Elemiah
Mahasiah
Lelahel
Achaiah
Cahethel
Haziel
Aladiah
Lauiah
Hahiah
Iezalel
Mebahel
Hariel
Hakamiah
Leviah
Caliel
Leuuiah
Pahaliah
Nelchael
Ieiaiel
Melahel
Hahuiah
Nithhaiah
Haaiah
Ierathel
Seehiah
Reiiel
Omael
Lecabel
Vasariah
Iehuiah
Lehahiah
Chavakiah
Monadel
Aniel
Haamiah
Rehael
Ihiazel
Hahahel
Michael
Vevaliah
Ielahiah
Sealiah
Ariel
Asaliah
Mihael
Vehuel
Daniel
Hahasiah
Imamiah
Nanael
Nithael
Mebahiah
Poiel
Nemamiah
Ieilael
Harahel
Mizrael
Umabel
Iahhel
Annauel
Mehekiel
Damabiah
Meniel
Eiael
Habuiah
Roehel
Iibamiah
Haiaiel
Mumiah
F. Barrett Del.
R. Griffith Sculp.

Fig. 29. The Shemhamphorash.

The use of the Shemhamphorash evolved in the quiet sanctuaries of the schools as a meditative aid for those engaged in the spiritual life, where it had long been understood that through using divine names in meditation one could utilise powerful spiritual forces to assist spiritual development. In this context

כהת Adorandus	אבא Longanimus	ללה Annunciatus	מהש Quæsitus	עלמ Salus	סיט Spes	ילי Auxilator	והו Exaltator
הקם Advocatus	הרי Ens	מבה Sublevator	יזל Decantatus	ההע Opportunus	לאו Exultabundus	אלד	הזי Recordabilis
ההו Expetendus	מלה Custos	ייי Dexter	נלב Fortia	פהל Ervens	לוו Exauditor	כלי Justitia	לאו Dominator
ושר Rector	לבב Solus	ארמ Adolescentia	רײ Sanator	שאה Festinus	ירת Salvator	האא Invocandus	נתה Mirabilis
ייז Propulsator	רהע Adivtor	העמ Refugium	אני Facies	מנד Gloria	כוק Deprecatio	להה Expectatio	יהו Cogitabundus
מיה Revelator	עשל Magnificus	ערי Operator	סאל Compatiens	ילה Doctor	וול Matutinus	מיכ Custos	ההה Liberator
פוי Erector	מבה Aeternum	נית Regnator	ננא Verus	עממ Altissimus	ההש Lætabundus	דני Clemens	והו Maximus
מהי Mercator	ענו Laudabilis	יהה Amabilis	ומב Benedictus	מצר Justus	הרח Oriens	ייל Animus	נממ Protector
מימ Requies	היי Multus	יבמ Deus	ראה Præmium	הבו Bonus	איע Dator	מנק Assisteus	דמב Deprecabilis

Fig. 30. The Shemhamphorash according to Christian D. Ginsburg.

they were also understood to be the names of the angels of Jacob's ladder, which reached from earth to heaven. In late medieval times, the use of the Shemhamphorash became central to the emerging interest in all things magical, and some or all of the seventy-two names were often used in magical rituals and or placed on medals or rolls of parchment to form talismans. However, it should be noted that it is not necessary to utter the names aloud in complex rituals to achieve spiritual benefits from them; there is as great, if not a greater possibility of being drawn closer to the essence of the name through an attentive application of consciousness in contemplation.

The composition of the name is derived from verses nineteen, twenty, and twenty-one of the fourteenth chapter of Exodus. Each of these verses contains seventy-two letters; the seventy-two names are formed by first writing down the letters of verse nineteen in correct order, then under them writing the letters of verse twenty in reverse order, and finally, writing down the letters of verse twenty-one under verse twenty in correct order. Reading them from the top down, we obtain seventy-two three-letter names, to each of which are appended the letters AL or III to form the seventy-two names of the Shemhamphorash.

THE LETTERS AND THE TAROT

In the late 18th century, the French scholar Court de Gebelin declared that the twenty-two trumps of the tarot were mystical emblems derived from the esoteric schools of Ancient Egypt. In the first volume of his book *Le Monde Primitif*, published in 1781, he stated his belief that the twenty two trump cards of the tarot were the vestige of an Ancient Egyptian book of wisdom called *The Book of Thoth*. Unfortunately, the truth is that as yet the origin of these cards is still unknown.

That they existed in the early fifteenth century is a matter of fact, but prior to this little can be said about them with any degree of certainty. It is generally accepted that the oldest surviving tarot cards are those known as the Bembo deck, so called because it is thought that they were painted by Bonifacio Bembo of Cremona for the Visconti-Sforza family of Milan sometime during the early 1440s. Whether or not they were created as vehicles of mystical knowledge is unknown.

What is also a matter of fact is that over the past two centuries a great deal of speculation has emerged concerning the origin and purpose of the tarot. The earliest specific reference from an esoteric point of view is that of Court de Gebelin. Other scholars believe that the tarot was brought into Europe by returning Crusaders, or at least was derived from Saracen sources. Paul Foster Case put forward a theory in his book, *The Tarot: A Key to the Wisdom of the Ages*, that about the year 1200, wise men from many parts of the world converged upon the city of Fez, Morocco, and met to discuss the ancient wisdom. In order to overcome the problems of language they prepared a pictorial book, which eventually became the emblematic pages of the tarot. Giovanni Covelluzzo, a 15th-century chronicler, claimed in his *History of Viterbo*, that the tarot cards were brought into Viterbo from the country of the Saracens in 1379. One particularly interesting association is that of the Sufi tradition. F. L. Cartwright, in his book *The Mystic Rose from the Garden of the King*, gives an account of a mystical treatise that has many correspondences with the tarot as we know it today. This treatise, incidentally, is thought to predate the Crusades by several centuries.

Many other theories exist concerning the origin of the tarot; some maintain that Indian chess lies at the root of the tarot, while others favour Chinese origins. The fact is that there is no real evidence to support any of these theories.

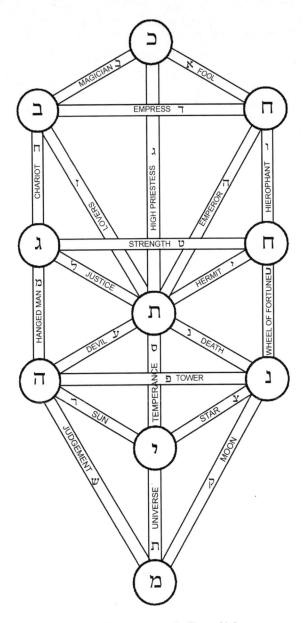

Fig. 31. An arrangement of the tarot on the Tree of Life.

Nevertheless, from the time of Court de Gebelin, the twenty-two trumps of the tarot have been attributed with bearing a secret mystical teaching; and from the time of Éliphas Lévi this mystical teaching has been connected with the twenty-two letters of the Hebrew alphabet.[10] This connection is certainly evident in the tarot trumps designs created in the mid-nineteenth century by Éliphas Lévi, and subsequently in those created by members of the Hermetic Order of the Golden Dawn and its various off-shoots; these did undoubtedly contain an exclusive esoteric teaching. One such initiate reported to me that the most important purpose of the tarot is, 'The revelation of the Secret Doctrine', a secret doctrine that was exclusive to the initiates of those orders.

A 19th-century example of a prototype for an English tarot deck that was never published, and which predated any published tarot deck in Britain, consisted simply of letters of the Hebrew alphabet with brief explanations appended for each of the four worlds.[11] The explanations were cryptic references to the more arcane aspects of the Sepher Yetzirah and suggested a profound understanding of the principles of a system of spiritual development little known outside the parameters of the Tradition. The same cannot be said with any certainty of the multitude of cards that bear the name of 'tarot' that have been published from the mid-twentieth century to the present day. It is probably true to say that none of the cards that have ever been published and made available to the general public embody anything beyond the vague use of occult symbols and images.

However, it should be noted that iconic images have been used continually throughout history for the edification of society and societies alike. One series that comes to mind

---

[10] Lévi was the first to identify the tarot trumps with the twenty-two letters of the Hebrew alphabet in his *Dogme et Rituel de la Haute Magie*, 1856.

[11] This tarot deck was designed by and for Frederick Holland, a 19th century-Rosicrucian and alchemist.

Table 6. The attribution of the Hebrew letters to the twenty-two tarot trumps has been a matter of some disagreement; what follows is but one example.

0	א	**Fool**	Idea, thought, spirituality
1	ד	**Magician**	Skill, wisdom, adaptation, craft
2	ג	**High Priestess**	Change, increase and decrease
3	ד	**Empress**	Beauty, happiness, pleasure, success
4	ו	**Emperor**	War, conquest, strife, ambition
5	ז	**Hierophant**	Divine wisdom, explanation
6	ח	**Lovers**	Inspiration and impulse
7	ט	**Chariot**	Triumph, victory, health
8	י	**Strength**	Courage, strength, fortitude
9	כ	**Hermit**	Wisdom from above
10	ל	**Wheel of Fortune**	Good fortune and happiness
11	מ	**Justice**	Eternal Justice and balance
12	נ	**Hanged Man**	Enforced sacrifice, punishment, loss
13	ס	**Death**	Time, ages, transformation, change
14	ע	**Temperance**	Combination of forces, realization
15	פ	**Devil**	Materiality, material force, temptation
16	צ	**Tower**	Ambition, fighting, war, courage
17	ק	**Star**	Hope, faith, unexpected help
18	ר	**Moon**	Dissatisfaction, voluntary change
19	ש	**Sun**	Glory, gain, riches, arrogance
20	ת	**Judgement**	Final decision, Judgement
21	ת	**Universe or World**	The matter itself, synthesis, world, kingdom

is the Stations of the Cross, which have been used by the Roman Catholic Church as aids in meditation much in the same way as a mandala or thangka may be used in Buddhism. Like all symbols, their capacity to provide inspiration is almost infinite. Another example, and probably more pertinent to our subject is the Masonic tracing board. There are in fact several, each designed as a focal point of instruction for one of the three degrees of Craft Masonry. Their symbolism embodies different levels of teaching for the appreciation of different levels of understanding. It is in the use of such devices that we may find the basis of the 'Secret Tradition' embedded in eighteenth and 19th-century tarot. The illustration of the 'Second Degree Tracing Board' (figure 32, p. 99) is a pictorial representation of some of the core doctrines of Freemasonry. It presents to the candidate an illustration of the interior of a three-story building. The candidate is asked to consider the image as a representation of the lodge and of the work undertaken therein. At the entrance stand two pillars, Jachin and Boaz. They are each surmounted by a globe, one of which is a terrestrial globe, the other a celestial globe, suggesting two worlds of experience and endeavour. Within is a curved flight of stairs that leads to the second floor. At the foot of the stairs stands a doorman or guardian. At the top of the stairs is another doorway that leads into another chamber, apparently illuminated by a great light. A doorman or guardian also attends this doorway. The whole image represents a movement away from the outer world of the senses to the inner kingdom of the soul.

The candidate must enter the interior world through the pillars of Jachin and Boaz, suggesting that the inner reality of the soul may only be comprehended through the harmonious integration of the principles they represent; this is not an easy undertaking. In Kabbalistic terms these principles are to be understood in terms of the masculine and feminine

Fig. 32. The Second Degree Tracing Board of Craft Freemasonry by John Harris, 1845.

potencies of the Supernals operating at all levels of creation. As the candidate progresses in the work, his understanding of these potencies and his ability to work with them evolves, as does his responsibility for his actions. To assist in this development the candidate is instructed to apply the faculty of reason to the cultivation of worthy thoughts, words, and deeds, for spiritual progress is dependent upon it. Thus the guardian at the foot of the stairs may be said to represent the part of the mind that watches over our thoughts, words, and actions in this world, that they may never offend God, society, or conscience. The guardian, then, corresponds with the application of will and reason operating in accordance with a rule of life, rather than reacting to the appetites and demands of the animal nature.

The curved stairway, otherwise known as the 'winding stair', embodies steps or stages of the candidate's progress. In some of the primitive Tracing Boards there are only seven steps—reflecting the cosmic dimensions of this work—in others, such as this one, there are fifteen: seven relate to the seven liberal arts and sciences that constitute the basic platform of the candidate's education. They also relate to the seven officers of the lodge who embody certain qualities of consciousness that the candidate will in due course develop. Five refer to the five classical orders of architecture and three correspond to the three archetypal characters that play a central role in the allegorical mythology of Freemasonry and to the three degrees of Freemasonry that the candidate will pass through to achieve the status of Master Mason.

Having ascended this staircase, the candidate may then enter the middle chamber where, tradition informs us, the Fellow Craftsmen working upon the great temple of King Solomon received their wages. This notion is extremely suggestive, alluding in part to the laws of causality that affect all living things and thus to the importance of living a whole-

some life according to the law, both spiritual and tempo-
ral. The guardian who stands at the entrance of the middle
chamber represents the will of the candidate no longer under
the influence of the mundane world and the animal nature,
but rooted in self-knowledge and understanding. The symbolism that has consciously been embedded in this image is
almost inexhaustible. It is well worth while taking the time
to explore it.

Chapter 4

The Soul

A GREAT DEAL OF Kabbalistic doctrine is concerned in one way or another with the nature, experience, and destiny of the soul. Yet, although many authors, both ancient and modern, have engaged with the psychology of the soul, few have really explained what they actually mean by the word. Some refer to the soul in terms of it being an entity; that such and such a person is a young or old soul; others refer to it in terms of it being a vehicle: my soul is filled with joy or love. But still the question remains: What is meant by the term 'soul?' The general consensus treats the soul as being the life-principle by which we think, will, know, and feel. Some believe that this principle is of an entirely non-material and spiritual nature, whilst others think of it as a material substance, a simple by-product of the chemistry of matter. Some attribute to it immortality, others believe it to be no more than mortal. Some think of it being a simple undifferentiated creature incapable of division, while others see it as a creature of many parts. For example, the ancient Egyptians believed that a person possessed a physical body (*Khat*), and an immaterial double of the body known as the *Ka*.[1] Furthermore, the *Ka* was also associated with the *Ba*,

---

[1]   For Egyptian beliefs in this field see E. A. Wallis Budge, *Egyptian Book of the Dead*. See also Budge, *Osiris and the Egyptian Resurrection*, vol. II (New York: Dover Publications, 1973) p. 134.

which was understood to reside within the heart. The *Ka* and the *Ba* dwelled in the tomb with the body, and were able to wander away from the body. Their continued existence, however, depended upon offerings being made by family and friends of the deceased. The existence of the *Ka* and the *Ba* was understood to come to an end eventually when offerings ceased. The permanent life-giving principle was the *Khu*, a term that means something like 'spirit-soul', whose nature was understood to be unchangeable, incorruptible, and immortal. When the body died, it was possible to raise up from it, by means of religious ceremonies, a spirit-body called a Sahu, which the Khu would inhabit and enter heaven to live with Osiris and the blessed for all eternity. There are other views concerning the apparently very complex psychology of the ancient Egyptians.

In Hinduism the Sanskrit word for the soul is *atman*, a word that means breath or wind, a correspondence that appears to be almost universal. The atman is regarded as a fragment or particle of the divine, and as such is understood to have divine attributes; thus it is eternal, without magnitude, and indestructible. The atman is often confused with the *jiva*, which is the vitalizing element in all living things, affected by phenomena and subject to the transitory effects of the sensitive life, such as pain and pleasure, whereas the atman is the permanent substrate of the individual.

To the people of ancient Greece the soul was commonly known as Psyche, which besides meaning breath, life, and spirit, also means butterfly or moth, a motif frequently used in ancient Greece as an emblem of the immortal soul. In the late Hellenic world it was held that the soul descended to earth from the heights of heaven, and that as it descended it was first clothed in an ethereal garment of nonmaterial purity; as it continued its descent through the planetary spheres, it received first a solar garment then a lunar garment. Finally it was born into a physical body. Alternatively, the followers of Orpheus understood that man consisted of two distinct natures: a mortal, physical nature, derived from the Titans[2] and an immortal spiritual nature derived from Dionysus. From this principle they taught that the soul must free itself by sublimating the passionate titanic nature and regenerating the divine Dionysian nature that lies within. In both cases the soul must shed the garments of the body to realise its own pristine nature.

Among Christians the most popular view today is that a person consists of an immortal soul and a mortal body. Many Christian theologians maintain that a fully developed soul is infused into the embryo at conception. However, opinions concerning this do vary; the constitution and formation of the soul has been the subject of a long and continuing debate. In the first century, St. Paul taught that man consisted of a mortal terrestrial body and an immortal celestial body. He writes, 'The first man was of the earth, made of dust; the second man is the Lord from heaven. As was the man of dust, so also are those who are made of dust; and as is the heavenly man, so also are those who are heavenly. And as we have borne the image of the man of dust, we shall also bear the image of the heavenly Man'.[3] In the first half of the third century, Origen taught that the soul existed in heaven, before Adam, and before descending into the world; that its imprisonment in a physical body was the result of a primeval fall from grace; and that the resurrection will not involve a

---

[2] In ancient Greek mythology, Dionysos was the son of Zeus by Persephone. His wife Hera resented Dionysos and sought to destroy him. This was accomplished with the aid of her own children, the Titans, who with childish toys lured him away to a place of ambush, where they tore him apart and ate him. Upon discovering this heinous crime Zeus destroyed the Titans with his thunderbolts. They were burnt to ashes, and from these very ashes humanity sprang up. Thus were our ancestors taught that human nature consists of the dark, destructive nature of the Titans, and the light, creative, and divine nature of Dionysos.

[3] I Corinthians 15: 47–49.

physical body. Against this, Tertullian argued that souls were contained in Adam, and that they were passed on to children from their parents in an act of material generation. Augustine held a similar opinion to that of Tertullian, except for him the generation was a spiritual generation. This doctrine is known as Traducianism.

Scholastic philosophers, as exemplified by Thomas Aquinas in the thirteenth century, understood the soul to be composed of a spiritual substance, and that it incarnated in three progressive stages of development: vegetative, sensitive, and rational. The first, the vegetative stage, corresponds with conception and the earliest development of the embryo; the second, the sensitive stage, emerges as the embryo develops; and the third, the rational stage, manifests as the embryo reaches maturity in the womb and completes the process of incarnation. These stages are consistent with Aquinas' assertion that three things are to be found in spiritual substances: Essence, Power, and Operation.[4] It is a notion that is comparable with the Hypostases of Neoplatonic thought; Essence corresponding with the One, Power with Nous, and Operation with the World Soul. Indeed, the influence of Neoplatonism is to be found in the doctrines of medieval Kabbalah and is in keeping with the doctrines taught in many esoteric Christian circles. This doctrine can be traced back to the teachings of Plato, who maintained that all souls existed before incarnating in a body, and that they exist for all eternity. These ideas are also expressed in Kabbalistic thought, which maintains that the soul was formed before the beginning of the world, hidden in the Divine; as the process of creation began, souls were brought forth into the upper paradise and stored in a great 'Treasure-house' (Binah), from whence they progressed into this world.

Over the course of time, Jewish theology has expressed many different views on the nature and destiny of the soul.

---

[4] Thomas Aquinas, *Summa Theologia* vol. 1 (New York: Christian Classics, 1981), Question 75, p. 363.

The classical and most enduring view is that of the Resurrection; which is the belief that at the end of the age the dead will be revived by God, complete with their bodies, to live again on earth. The biblical view of the Resurrection is best summed up in Daniel 12:2–3, where it says, 'And many of them that sleep in the dust of the earth shall awake, some to everlasting life and some to reproach and everlasting shame. And the wise shall shine as the brightness of the firmament and some of the many righteous as the stars for ever and ever'. This doctrine encapsulates two basic conceptions. The first suggests the unity of body and soul; two equal components of humanity. The second proposes a moral dimension that determines the nature of post-resurrection existence. However, the Bible is not absolutely clear about the posthumous fate of the soul—the most distinct view expressed being that the soul descends into a kind of Hades called *Sheol*,[5] wherein it leads a vague, ethereal, and shadowy existence. During the time of the Second Temple, the concept of an immortal, posthumous existence in the heavenly realms arose, and competed with the more traditional concept of the resurrection of the dead. Eventually, the belief in the immortality of the soul became a fundamental principle of both the Jewish and Christian faiths.

In the Talmudic period the rabbis generally taught that the soul was separable from the body (Gen. 2:7); separating during sleep to draw nourishment from the spiritual realms and, at death, leaving the body only to be reunited with it again at the Resurrection. At the same time, some of the rabbis taught that after death a righteous soul entered the Garden of Eden and that wicked souls went to Gehinnom;[6] or that righteous souls ascended upward,

---

[5]   *Sheol*, literally, 'the pit', sometimes 'catacombs'. In English translations it usually reads as 'hell'. See Genesis 37:35, where *Sheol* is translated as 'grave'.

[6]   Gehinnom, a valley lying southwest of Jerusalem, was where children were sacrificed to the gods Baal and Moloch. Since rabbinic times the term describes the after-death place of torment for the wicked.

to be gathered into the Treasury, while wicked souls were cast back upon the earth—in other words, they were subject to reincarnation; opinions about this have differed from time to time, and place to place.

The Hebrew word for reincarnation or the transmigration of souls is *Gilgul*. However, it should be noted that Talmudic tradition does not overtly acknowledge this doctrine, although later mystics have interpreted various rabbinical texts as allegories suggesting it. On the other hand, Kabbalistic doctrine does clearly support and teach the transmigration of souls. Gilgul is evident in the Bahir, the earliest of the medieval Kabbalistic texts, in which several passages refer to the transmigration of souls. For example:

> Why is there a righteous person who has good, and [another] righteous person who has evil? This is because the [second] righteous person was wicked previously, and is now being punished. Is one then punished for his childhood deeds? Did not Rabbi Simon say that in the Tribunal on high, no punishment is meted out until one is twenty years or older. He said: I am not speaking of his present lifetime. I am speaking about what he has already been, previously.[7]

The Bahir was not unique in holding this position on transmigration. But it should be noted that among medieval Kabbalists the teachings concerning transmigration were quite narrow and generally confined to specific circumstances. Not every soul was subject to transmigration, but only those for whom it was absolutely necessary. It was taught that the righteous—those who had fulfilled their obligations as Jews—had no need to reincarnate, whereas, the majority of souls, those who had failed in their obligations, and were therefore to some degree sinners, became subject to the process of transmigration. The incorrigibly wicked, alas, were to be condemned to the fires of

---

[7]   Aryeh Kaplan, trans. *The Bahir: Illumination* (York, ME: Weiser, 1979), p. 77, verse 195.

hell. It was also taught that the number of incarnations was generally limited to three. This notion is clearly drawn from the Book of Job, where it states: 'Behold, God works all these things twice, in fact three times with a man to bring back his soul from the Pit that he may be enlightened with the light of life'.[8] However, it was also understood that the righteous are the zaddik,[9] who are souls sent by God with the ability to reincarnate many times for the benefit of the world. Kabbalistic doctrine maintains that the soul is a spiritual entity whose origin is divine and whose immortal nature is an incontrovertible fact, and that it incarnates in the world only to fulfil a specific task; the fulfilment of which enables it to engage in a many-staged ascent to its primal dwelling place. This ascent begins with the soul attaining entrance to the earthly paradise, from where it begins its ascent. The teaching concerning the soul's role in this work is central to Kabbalism.

Although the soul is essentially one thing it may be divided into several distinct parts. This is clearly demonstrated in the Zohar where the prevailing view is that the soul consists of three parts: the *Nephesh*, *Ruach*, and *Neshemah* (see figure 33, page 113). Gershom Scholem states that the early Kabbalists knew of only three parts to the soul, and it was only at a later date that further refinements took place in schools such as Safed.[10] Subsequent schools have identified more varied and complex divisions.

The term *Nephesh* refers to the part of the soul that is associated with the body and all of those things connected with sustaining our physical being throughout life. It is not the

---

[8] Job 33:29-30.

[9] Zaddik, a 'righteous one'; in Hasidism the zaddik is a saint, a living embodiment of the Torah. See Scholem, *Major Trends in Jewish Mysticism*, p. 344.

[10]   Scholem, *On the Mystical Shape of the Godhead*, p. 230. Safed is a town in upper Galilee that became a centre of rabbinic and Kabbalistic activity. From 1530 onward Safed became the focal point of a Jewish spiritual renaissance. Here, between 1530 and 1590, emerged a distinctive Kabbalistic world view and religious way of life, formed in the main through the influence of Joseph Karo, Moses ben Jacob Cordovero, and Isaac Luria.

body itself, but the lowest expression of the spiritual life of the soul. Its nature is to fulfil the needs of the flesh and to preserve it from harm; it is appetitive and driven to survive at all costs. It has no light or energy of its own but receives its sustenance from the Ruach. Although its responsibility is to the physical body it is attributed to the world of Yetzirah and corresponds with the etheric body. The term 'Ruach' refers to the faculty of consciousness associated with the principle of rational thought. It is through the Ruach that the soul is sustained. If the life force of the Ruach were to be withdrawn then death would ensue because the Nephesh would be unable to maintain itself in the body. The Ruach is attributed to the world of Briah and corresponds with the spiritual body, but for most of humanity it is a spiritual body subject to the vicissitudes of the passionate nature. The term 'Neshamah' refers to the spiritual faculty of the soul. It is the sovereign reason within us, which is the true spiritual intellect above the rational mind. It is hewn from the source of life and from the wellspring of intelligence and wisdom, and is attributed to the world of Atziluth.

That all exist as part of one thing is unquestionable, but few in this world are able to take advantage of the powers of all three. It is said that every soul is conscious at the level of Nephesh; however, it is taught that if it is used well, to its highest potential, then consciousness of the Ruach is bestowed upon the soul.[11] If the soul is also able to use the Ruach to its highest purpose then the divine Godhead exalts the soul, bestowing upon it the crown of Neshamah. It is the objective of all true seekers, for it is through the power of the Neshamah that the Ruach is emancipated from the shackles of the mundane world and thus able to realise its true spiritual nature. Other names attributed to it are the Higher Self, the Overself, and the Holy Guardian Angel of the soul. These attributions, however, should not

---

[11] The soul is invited into the house of the Ruach, as it were.

be confused with the concept of the *Tselem*, which notion-
ally, at least, corresponds with the astral body. In medieval
Kabbalistic thought the Higher Self, or true spiritual self,
was attributed to the Tselem. This concept is based on Genesis 1:26, where it states: 'Then God said, let Us make man,
in our image, according to our likeness'. However, the Zohar
regards the Tselem as the etheric or astral body that serves as
the intermediary between the soul and the physical body. It
was thought that because the nature of the Neshamah and
the Nephesh were too removed from each other to form a
proper bond, the Tselem was created, woven, as it were, as a
garment from man's previous good deeds. Thereby illustrat-
ing a deeper teaching concerning how significant morality
and obedience to the Torah was to the soul's ongoing existence. This etheric form was considered to be our true form,
which could only be revealed to the purified spiritual sight
of the dedicated Kabbalist.

The distinction between the Neshamah, our essential
spiritual individuality, and the Tselem is that the Tselem
is the vehicle—the form, not the essence—through which
the will of the Neshamah is manifest, its primary purpose
being to serve as a mold, or pattern, for the physical body.
It is better known today as the etheric body. It is also the
vehicle through which other unnatural and perverse forces
and entities of the *Klippoth* may manifest themselves. Innu-
merable magical texts, particularly from medieval times, are
concerned with invoking this vehicle or form to serve purposes for which it was not intended, and for which there is
invariably a terrible cost to pay. Concerning which it is said:
'Invoke not the visible Image of the Soul of Nature'.[12]

There is a tradition, albeit one that arose much later than
the Zohar, of attributing the letters of the Tetragrammaton
to different levels of the soul (see figure 34 on page 115). This
requires dividing the soul into four distinct parts, the highest

---

[12]   W. W. Westcott, *Chaldean Oracles of Zoroaster* (See *Collectanea Hermetica*
[York, ME: Weiser, 1998], p. 46), verse 149.

of which is the *Yehidah*. Much of what we have contemplated so far concerning the Neshamah is attributed in this scale to the Yehidah. Concerning this method of attribution Arthur Edward Waite states:

> There is also a correspondence between the four let-ters of the Tetragrammaton and certain diverse parts or aspects of the soul in man.
>
>   The letter ' = YOD is in analogy with YEHIDAH, a spiritual state or mode in the ascending scale of inward being, and with all that is postulated above it, the human singularitas, the Christian apex of the soul and Divine Selfhood. The ה = HE primal answers to NESHAMAH the sovereign reason within us, above material mind; the ו = VAU connects with RUA'H which is the normal intellectuality, the rational prin-ciple; and the ה HE final with NEPHESH, the side on which humanity is related to the animal world. It is the lower vitalitas, and is not as such the physical body, which is, however, its vehicle.[13]

There is another perspective that perceives the soul as being divided into five distinct parts. According to the Kabbalah of Isaac Luria, there are five worlds: the first is that of the Adam Kadmon, the rest follow the traditional system of the four worlds—Atziluth, Briah, Yetzirah, and Assiah. Accordingly Yehidah is allocated to the world of Adam Kadmon. In human terms the Yehidah is the essential self, the quintessence of the human personality. *Chiah* is attributed to Atziluth; in us it is the real life-principle, the vitalitas, as distinct from the more illusionary life of the physical body. Neshamah is attributed to Briah, Ruach, to Yetzirah, and the Nephesh, to Assiah. Another variation is based on the Tree of Life being divided into two sections: an upper and a lower. The upper section corresponds to the spiritual dimension of the soul and the lower to the physical. Thus: to Kether is attributed Yehidah, to Chokmah is

---

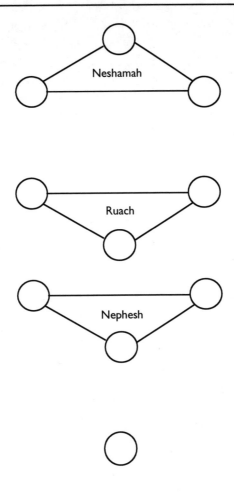

Fig. 33. Distribution of the soul on the Tree of Life according to the Zohar.

attributed Chiah, to Binah is attributed Neshamah, to Chesed is attributed the Ruach, and to Geburah is attributed the Nephesh. Rabbi Azriel of Gerona maintains the same concept but with different attributions. He assigned the Ruach to Binah, the Nephesh to Chesed, and the Neshamah to Geburah. There are other attributions, many of which are confusing to anyone but those initiated into their use.

From both a Jewish and a Christian Kabbalistic perspective, the soul is in a fallen state and must rise out of it; this is the principal work of the Kabbalist, to regenerate and reintegrate the soul; both of the individual and of humanity itself. The first step in achieving this objective, as is the primary work of spiritual aspirants everywhere, lies in undertaking the work of self-improvement, whereby one may participate in the great work of spiritual regeneration. In the Christian mysteries, the path of the soul's spiritual perfection may be understood as consisting of seven stages, thus:

1. Purification of the senses, appetites and desires;
2. Control of the tongue;
3. Examination and purification of conscience;
4. Prayer;
5. Meditation on the maxims of faith;
6. Development of virtue;
7. Frequent Communion.

It is no different for initiates in any other faith or philosophy. Indeed, the same kind of work is undertaken by the apprentice Freemason, who is likened to a rough stone freshly taken from the quarry, and who must be shaped into the perfect cube before he is fit for use in the construction of the Temple; the analogy being that until his mind and nature are sufficiently

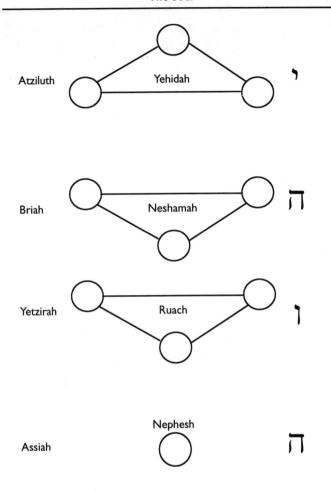

Fig. 34. Fourfold distribution of the soul on the Tree of Life.

refined he will be unable to engage in the spiritual work. The same may be recognised in the labours of the initiates of the mystery schools of the Greco-Roman world. Before undertaking the Cathartic rites, they must first develop the civic virtues, moderating their passions and learning to live in harmony with society. These same virtues—prudence, fortitude, justice, and temperance, are also the basis for the essential work of spiritual regeneration.

Thus it is that the Talmud instructs those who have the eyes to see that the process of spiritual regeneration begins with purifying the instinctive nature of the Nephesh. Aryeh Kaplan informs us that there are ten steps outlined in the Talmud that if followed diligently, will enable the soul to purify the Nephesh; these are:

1. Study;
2. Carefulness;
3. Diligence;
4. Cleanliness;
5. Abstention;
6. Purity;
7. Piety;
8. Humility;
9. Fear of sin;
10. Holiness.[14]

The completion of these preparatory steps enables the soul to engage with work that is invariably far too refined for a mind otherwise steeped in the animal nature of the Nephesh. Such a soul, having struggled in the outer halls of discipline understands the real meaning of the words: 'Receive instruction, and not silver; and knowledge rather than tried gold. For Wisdom is better than precious stones; and no valuable substance is of equal worth to it'.[15] Those who have laboured

---

[14]   Aryeh Kaplan, *Meditation and the Bible* (York, ME: Weiser, 1988), p. 20.
[15]   Proverbs 8:10–11.

thus, find themselves in a state of consciousness that enables them to enter into the silent depths of their being and engage in the work of a Kabbalist. Indeed, the point cannot be emphasised too much that the work of the Kabbalist is an interior work that uses the rational mind as a launching point toward spiritual integration and understanding. The main objective is not the elevation of consciousness but the transformation of the nature of consciousness. It goes without saying that the study of the scriptures along with other relevant material is an important part of the work. However, without the discipline of prayer and meditation, such studies are merely an intellectual exercise.

Chapter 5

Meditation

IT IS PROBABLE that the earliest system of spiritual development in Israel took the form of emulating Moses' ascent of the sacred mountain of Sinai. This ascent is described in the Book of Exodus, the second book of the Pentateuch, which forms part of the oral tradition put into writing during the Babylonian captivity. It describes how the Jewish people, led by Moses, escaped from the land of Egypt. This narrative can be read as an analogy concerning the passage of the soul out of the mundane world, which is the body and the animal nature; thus Egypt represents the bondage of the soul to the demands of the animal or instinctive animal nature—the mundane world. The Pentateuch consists of five books that among other things describe:

1. The creation and fall of the soul
2. The wandering of the soul in the world
3. The soul's enslavement and liberation from
   Egypt
4. Humanity's entry into the wilderness and the
   pilgrimage to the holy mountain
5. Moses' ascent of the holy mount

6. The covenant between God and the soul
7. The re-alignment of the soul with divine law
8. The soul's entry into the promised land

The Creation may be understood in metaphorical terms as the creation of the human soul, an immortal being whose only vesture is a garment of pure spirit, or perhaps of light. In this state the soul exists within the presence of God (Paradise), all needs fulfilled by that divine presence. Here time and space have no place, all share in the unity and omniscience of God. The fall is a descent out of the divine presence into the material world of duality and all that such implies where the soul experiences birth and death, pain and suffering, the needs of the flesh, and the need to work to survive; but worst of all, separation from the presence of God and the darkness of ignorance that comes with it. Consequently the wandering of the people of Israel in this world signifies the soul's growing awareness of this transient world. In its fallen state, the soul knows nothing and has nothing, other than what the senses show and bring to it. Thus it engages with the world it perceives via the senses, and to which it is driven by the incessant demands of the animal nature of the body. This animal or instinctive nature is by and large an unrelenting taskmaster and is symbolically represented by Egypt (the world) and Pharaoh, the personality as an embodiment of our appetites. And thus the destiny of the soul would be irrevocably fixed if it were not for the influence of the divine through the agency of Moses. Moses represents the human will that has touched the heavenly realm and been inspired by the presence of God (as in the burning bush). Thus inspired, the will is able to comprehend the limitations of the world of the senses, and thus able to overcome the instinctive nature (Pharaoh), and gather his people (faculties) and withdraw them out of the immediate sphere of the instinctive nature.

The wilderness is a vast place neither in heaven nor on earth. It is the great unknown that must be crossed, symbolised in all of the great epics quests and journeys from Gilgamesh to the present. To the soul the wilderness is a vast astral region that is only accessed when it leaves the world of the senses. It is a world wherein many lose themselves. However, the people of Israel were led through the wilderness by a pillar of fire at night and a pillar of smoke by day to the holy mountain of Sinai. Now a mountain signifies a high place in consciousness; such heights are not to be understood literally but metaphorically, for they represent levels of consciousness not available to the sense-bound soul. In comparison the wilderness is a low place in consciousness that extends metaphorically to the four directions; north, south, east, and west, not to the heights, for the wilderness describes the uncontrollable aspects of the world of the senses, whereas the heights are symbolic of the heavenly realms, and Mount Sinai represents the high places of consciousness that the soul must ascend if it is to have any possibility of spiritual regeneration. Thus it is said that Moses (the will) is called by God (inspired) to ascend the mountain (to the heavenly realms). It is an ascent in consciousness beyond the world of the senses—beyond the world of the imagination, and even beyond the realm of abstract thought—into the presence of God, who establishes a new covenant with the soul. It is an interesting arrangement that requires of the soul that it recognise and accept the omnipresence and unity of the divine, that it turn away from investing the transient with power, and that it understand that all providence is from the divine, and that there is no need to hold on to the desire for possessions. It is essentially an arrangement that requires the soul to realign itself with divine law, for only then will it be able to enter the Promised Land—the presence of God—and fulfil its destiny. This, broadly speaking, is a Kabbalistic interpretation of the human condition set out in the five books of The Pentateuch.

The Kabbalah introduces the student to a deeper meaning of these books, the contemplation of which enables the beginning of spiritual understanding, and at the heart of which lies a teaching concerning the soul's path to freedom from the influences of the mundane world. This path is an interior journey into the depth of one's being; it is a difficult journey full of pitfalls, yet, when all is said and done, it is a path worth following, for at its terminus lies the emancipation of the soul. The beginning of this path is allegorically described in Exodus, under the following headings:

a.   The exodus of the Jewish people out of Egypt
b.   Their journey to the foot of Mount Sinai
c.   Moses's ascent of Mount Sinai

An important part of the work of a Kabbalist is to engage in the art and discipline of meditation, and although it is possible to engage in meditation simply for the purpose of relaxation, meditation is essentially a spiritual discipline, that enables the mind to be concentrated on a specific subject in a state of deep relaxation. For the Kabbalist, that subject is Scripture, the study of which is a profound engagement in meditation; and the most important tool in this engagement is a mind supported by a clear conscience and a willingness to engage with the work. To apply oneself effectively to the meditative exploration of Scripture requires background study and research, and, sufficient time to reflect upon the subject matter contained therein. The interior path that leads the individual into the deep recesses of the soul, beyond the normal parameters of biology and psychology, does not reveal itself easily; unrelenting persistence is absolutely necessary if progress is to be made. There is no easy path to proficiency in meditation, it is an art learned in the school of hard knocks, and much of the preliminary work of the Kabbalist is concerned with learning this art. Scripture reveals its inner meaning slowly. Consider the following simple example: the opening words of Genesis, the first book of the Bible, reads in English 'In the Beginning', and in Hebrew, *Bereshith*:

בראשית

In studying this word the following may be extrapolated: ברא, which means 'begin' or 'create'; ראש, which means 'head' or 'fount'; אש, which means 'fire' or 'existence'; שית, which means 'to prepare' or 'to place'; ראשית, which means 'starting point', 'first-fruit', 'first-born'. Furthermore, three pertinent transpositions or anagrams present themselves: איש, which means 'man'; בית, which means 'house'; and; בת, which means 'daughter'.

These words, contained within Bereshith allude to an inner meaning, suggesting to the Kabbalist that the head or fount of creation, the 'beginning' of all things, is Kether. Now, a fundamental tenet of Kabbalah is that Kether is the first point of Positive Existence, in which the divine light of AIN SOPh AUR is concentrated, and as such it is the fount or well-spring of creation. Thus our exegesis suggests that hidden within this head or fount is to be found the essence of all that will be in the form of a potential energy or primal fire אש, the nature of which is beyond comprehension but not beyond inference. This sacred fire flows through the Tree of Life energizing and sustaining the entire creation. Hidden in this fount lies the primordial man איש who, through the power of the divine will, is manifest as the archetype of the created universe (Chokmah), and creator of the world and all of the souls who will inhabit the world. And that the foundation of the created world is the daughter (Binah) whose house or palace בית is the well-spring of the souls of all living things. He is the creator of all; she is the maker and former of all. He is YHVH יהוה; she is YHVH ELOHIM יהוה אלהים. Both are part of the one thing.

The Zohar explores the scriptural references to the creation of two Adams given in the first and second chapters of Genesis. The first is understood by the Kabbalist to be the primordial man referred to above. This divine being is the full representation of our complete spiritual nature, an androgynous being not subject to mortality and all that such implies,; and of whose divine nature the mortal human has no comprehension. The whole Sephirotic realm, in the form of the Tree of Life, is a representation of this divine being who is known to the Kabbalist as Adam Kadmon, the archetypal man; and who may be contemplated thus: Kether as a crown sits upon or above his head while Chokmah and Binah form the two halves of the brain; Chesed and Geburah constitute the organs of action, the left and right arms; Tiphereth is the heart and the vital organs of the chest; while Netzach and Hod form the lower limbs. Yesod refers to the digestive and reproductive organs; lastly, Malkuth constitutes the feet or foundation of the first Adam, the archetypal man—Adam Kadmon (figure 35, p. 125).

Thus, from the opening words of the Bible we are able to comprehend in our meditation that a hidden teaching is to be found in the scriptures concerning an archetypal being, Adam Kadmon, who is created in the image of the hidden and unknowable God—En-Sof, and, who emerges out of the depths of that Godhead. Furthermore, that from Kether, the fount of divine and infinite potential, the entire creation is brought into being as an embodiment of that divine nature. There is far more that may be extrapolated from this opening word, far more than may be written here. It should be noted, however, that:

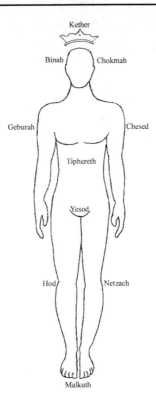

Fig. 35. Adam Kadmon.

- This method of extrapolation or exegesis is central to the
  Kabbalah of all ages and that the Zohar was written
  and compiled using it;
- This method is equally accessible to any individual,
  whether it be a humble beginner or a seasoned Kabbalist;
- That metaphor and allegory have often been used to
  conceal and reveal the deeper teachings contained
  within the scriptures.

One of the most significant figures to systematically use metaphor and allegory in interpreting scripture was Philo Judaeus,[1] an influential Jewish mystic and philosopher who was a contemporary of Jesus and St. Paul, and who lived in the Egyptian city of Alexandria during the first century A.D. Philo wrote seventy or more treatises concerning philosophy, religion, and the spiritual life. By far the majority of the fifty or so treatises that have survived are commentaries on Scripture, and many of these works are concerned with the symbolic or allegorical understanding of Scripture.[2]

Philo maintained that Moses compiled the Pentateuch in such a way that it could be understood allegorically, and that the literal interpretation was by itself insufficient to express the profound nature of Scriptures in its entirety. He declared that Moses signified that mind was a symbolic representation of heaven and that the intellect was essentially of a heavenly nature; that sensation was a symbolic representation of earth because it is of a corporeal nature. Thus, the things of heaven are perceived only by the intellect and the things of the earth by the external senses.[3] He further taught that humanity is of a two-fold nature; the first is a heavenly creature, who being created in the image of God did not participate directly in the natural world, whereas the earthly man was a creature of clay whose domain was the world of the senses. This allegorical method of interpretation was not unknown in the Hellenistic world, where it was generally used for developing a greater understanding of the Greek traditions, particularly Homer's works, and it is evident that Philo and his circle used it extensively.

His teachings are not considered to be unique but neither are they commonplace. That they were derived from a school within the Jewish mystical tradition is highly probable; such schools and their doctrines were tradition-

---

[1]   *ca.* 20 B.C. to *ca.* A.D. 50

[2]   Kenneth Schenck, *A Brief Guide to Philo* (Louisville, KY: W.J.K. Press, 2005), p. 14.

[3]   Yonge, trans., *The Works of Philo:, Allegorical Interpretations I*, p. 25.

ally closed to outsiders. Indeed, it is a notion that has been supported over the course of time by various scholars who have claimed that Philo's work was substantially derivative, suggesting that he was merely a transmitter of other people's thoughts. Whatever the truth of the matter it is known that he disseminated his teachings extensively and may well have established his own school in Alexandria, educating his fellow Jews in scriptural interpretation. His style, if not his influence, is to be seen, not only in the later Rabbinic and Talmudic texts, but also in the texts of some of the Christian Fathers, such as Origen. Furthermore, his methodology has been used extensively by Kabbalists throughout the history of the tradition. It is a method that is very useful in the work of meditation, providing interesting keys to otherwise impenetrable mysteries. Indeed, it enables the aspirant to develop the power of thinking laterally, especially when combined with the speculative tools of gematria, notarikon, and temurah (see pages 83–86).

THE ART OF MEDITATION

For many students the art of meditation seems to evade them; some find that when they first begin meditation they either become physically very uncomfortable or their minds become very active, more active than normal, bringing the endeavour to a frustrating halt. How then do we begin to understand and engage in meditation? Popular opinion invariably associates the practise of meditation with oriental religions and philosophies. Indeed, the archetypal image that presents itself to the imagination is not that of a venerable Kabbalist in meditation but a Buddhist monk or Indian sadhu sitting cross-legged on a cushion or low wooden stool, eyes closed and breathing slowly; possibly chanting or repeating a mantra. However, as true and romantic it may be, such an image would be very difficult to find in the environs of modern, industrialised nations. Indeed, the most popular methods of meditation to be found in the modern world are themselves products of the imagination of that world. They are essentially guided fantasies that derive more from a syncretic blend of spiritualism, yoga, Buddhism and shamanism than from any school of pure meditation, Eastern or otherwise. Most methods of guided fantasy can be traced back to the ideas and practises employed by nineteenth and early twentieth-century esoteric schools such as the Hermetic Order of the Golden Dawn. This particular Order was significant in that it was to become the model for the formation of a host of esoteric movements, most of which were deeply involved with the magical aspects of the Western Mystery Tradition—especially with astral projection and all that such implies: and it implies a great deal.

Looking back a little further, we can see how in the nineteenth century the emergence of these esoteric schools was an inevitable and natural expression of the interest in Hermetic and Rosicrucian thought and philosophy that evolved in seventeenth and eighteenth-century Europe. These schools were not merely a focus for the theoretical, but also for the essential practical workings of the Western Mystery Tradition. The nineteenth century also witnessed the return of ancestor worship in the form of spiritualism, and the emergence of the Theosophical Society, which sought to create a universal religion based upon oriental religious ideas such as those fostered by Buddhism. I mention this because it was through the activities of the Theosophical Society that Hinduism and Buddhism—particularly Tibetan Buddhism—became so accessible to Western civilisation. The high point of Theosophy was in the 1920s and 1930s. However, as was the case for many things, its growth and development was impeded by the drama of the World War II. Indeed, as the world began to recover from the effects of that war, the light of the Theosophical Society began to fade, just as popular interest in Hindu systems of yoga and meditation began to grow.

Shamanism, on the other hand, did not emerge in popular culture until the late twentieth century, and then only in a romanticised form; its popularity, perhaps, being due to its association with astral projection and channelling, subjects that have either fascinated or horrified humanity since time immemorial. Another significant contribution to the guided fantasy approach has come from the various psychodynamic processes that surfaced, particularly in America, from the mid-twentieth century onward. Although deeply influenced by the materialism of analytical psychology and behaviourism, and invariably defined in the psychological language of Sigmund Freud and Carl Gustav Jung, they are often to be found at the heart of many modern systems of self-development.

However, from a traditional and classical point of view, meditation is essentially a private and introspective process whereby, in a state of deep relaxation, the attention is concentrated upon a given theme. Over the course of the centuries many different methods of meditating have been developed, the majority of which are based on the premise that the discursive activities of the mind can be brought to a standstill by focussing the attention on one subject to the exclusion of all others. The simplest and probably the oldest method is that of observing the flow of the breath. In the schools the focal point of concentration is the Scriptures to which the wandering attention is always returned. The path of spiritual development through meditation leads to a greater understanding of the nature of experience and the chemistry of our consciousness through 'insight', a term used here to describe the ability of the mind to acquire a profound understanding of a subject through the sustained concentration of the attention upon it. This ability alone, which seemingly emerges only within the parameters of meditation, makes it a highly valuable discipline, especially in the work of Kabbalah.

A simple yet effective method that has been universally employed since ancient times is a method known simply as 'The Way' or 'The Ladder'. In more recent times, by which I mean from the sixth century onward, it came to be known as *lectio divina* or 'divine reading', and as such was used for the study of Scripture and as a basis for a graduated system of prayer. This method is an ancient spiritual discipline that was well known in the classical world before the advent of Christianity. It consists of the slow, repetitive reading of a passage of scripture until it is known by heart, followed by meditating on its significance. Traditionally, the reading, or *lectio*, is read aloud with the emphasis being upon the act of listening, and repeated time after time until the passage is known 'off by heart'. If the sacred text is to be read by another person it is important for those listening to repeat the words with their lips, under their breath, as it were. This listening is no mere act of hearing; rather it is an act of attending with the whole of one's mind, engaging as much of one's being in the reading as possible, thereby cultivating the ability to perceive something of the soul of the text. This attending, or listening, is called *meditatio,* or meditation.

The response to the meditatio was varied, but often took the form of spontaneous extemporary prayer, of communing with God or engaging in worship, singing hymns etc. This was known as *oratio.* At other times, *oratio* took the form of inspired writings that in some way related to the *lectio* and *meditatio.* Those who persevered with this discipline found that the oratio subsided into a quiet state of rest in what has been described as the presence of God and was tradition-

ally called *contemplatio*, or contemplation. *Lectio divina* is one
of the oldest methods of prayer known to humanity. It is
embodied in the works of Philo of Alexandria and is clearly
expressed in the work of the Pseudo-Dionysius particularly
in the book *On the Divine Names*. It was used extensively by
the early Church, but was enshrined in the Rule of St. Ben-
edict in the sixth century and became one of the distinctive
features of monastic life. Aryeh Kaplan describes just such a
method in *Meditation and the Bible*, published by Weiser in
1978, and still available as of this writing.

The Four Stages of 'The Way'

Allow sufficient time free from commitments to engage in
this work without haste; an hour will do. Wear loose comfortable clothing. This meditation should be done in a place
dedicated to this purpose, ideally in a consecrated or sacred
space, however, it may also be done in a domestic environment, but do choose a place that is clean and free from disturbance, i.e. people, telephones, noisy traffic, and so on. Sit
in a firm but comfortable chair, ensuring that your spine is
straight and that your head is balanced comfortably, without
leaning too far forward or backward.

Stage One

Having selected a short passage of text from Scripture, read
it slowly over and over again—aloud, if possible. Attend to
every word as you read it. Let your reading be slow and grace-
ful, synchronizing your speech with your breathing, which
should be slow, gentle, and easy. Continue in this manner
until you know it by heart, or for 10 to 15 minutes.

Stage Two

If you have been able to memorise the text, then repeat it internally and silently, reflecting on its significance. Otherwise, a word or phrase may have attracted your attention, then reflect on the significance of that word or phrase in the context of the reading. Continue in this vein for as long as you are moved, or for 10 to 15 minutes.

Stage Three

At some point in this exercise you may be inspired to write down or record your thoughts in response to the text; alternatively, you may choose to express your experience in prayer, in song or perhaps in paint: some of the world's greatest spiritual prose was inspired in this exalted state.

Stage Four

There comes a point when the most natural thing to do is to be still, to dwell in the silence. Within the depths of the silence, the soul may become aware of a sense of peace, a peace that becomes more and more manifest as it dwells therein. It is the first tangible experience that the soul has of the presence of the divine, and abiding in that presence is the basis of true contemplation and the bedrock of unshakable faith. The virtue of this ancient method is that it is simple, safe, and very adaptable. However, do not be deceived by its simplicity; it is not called The Way and The Ladder for nothing: it is both a preparation for and a part of ascending the Holy Mountain itself.

THE HOLY MOUNTAIN

The ascent of the holy mountain is an ancient motif that has been used in many cultures to describe the interior work of spiritual development. In ancient Egypt it was represented by the pyramid,[4] which is a symbol of the sacred mound that emerged out of the primal waters of Nut at the beginning of creation, and upon the apex of which perched the phoenix, the symbol of life and regeneration. In Babylon, the ziggurat (a stepped pyramid, sometimes spiral, but generally square) was a formal representation of the sacred mountain (see figure 36). Known as the 'House of the Shining Mountain', the ziggurat varied from three to seven platforms. Each of the platforms of a seven-stepped pyramid was dedicated to a planetary deity, and was often distinguished by a particular colour. Complex rituals evolved around the ascent of these platforms. The ziggurat was established upon the earth as a representation of the cosmos and the abode of the gods. It was designed and created as a means of reaching and observing the heavens, and communing with the gods. Sacrifices were offered at the base, where the congregation met. The shrine was to be found at the summit and was reached by ascending from platform to platform, doubtless honouring the planetary deity of each level until one reached the summit and communed with the supreme deity.

The concept of ascent and descent was given a very clear form of expression in the Greco-Roman world. It was com-

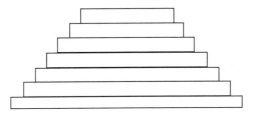

Fig. 36. Babylonian ziggurat.

---

[4]   The earliest Egyptian pyramids were stepped, as in Babylonia.

monly maintained that when the soul came down to earth it descended from the heavenly realm of the fixed stars through the planetary spheres accumulating an increasingly dense body and particular faculties from each planetary sphere.

Franz Cumont describes it thus:

> It was held that when the soul came down to earth it first received an ethereal garment of almost immaterial purity; then imagination being added to reason, a solar fluid surrounded it; then a lunar integument made it subject to the passions; and finally a carnal body was the cause of its ignorance of divine truths and of its blind foolishness.[5]

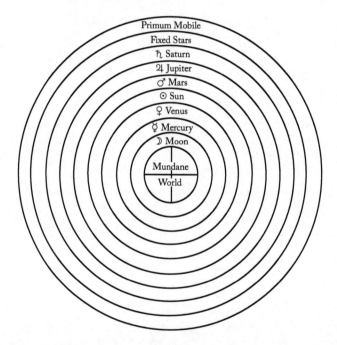

Fig. 37. Greco-Roman cosmological system; also a symbol of the Holy Mountain and, in later times, of the Tree of Life.

5   Franz Cumont, *After Life in Roman Paganism* (New Haven: Yale University Press, 1922), p. 106.

The return journey involved the soul passing through the same planetary zones, divesting itself of the attributes and faculties it had received during its descent. 'To the moon it surrendered its vital and alimentary energy, to Mercury its cupidity, to Venus its amorous desires, to the sun its intellectual capacities, to Mars its warlike ardour, to Jupiter its ambitious dreams, to Saturn its slothful tendencies'.[6] The ideas expressed by Franz Cumont, are to be found at the heart of many of the transcendental systems of the ancient world, and are equally reflected in Jewish mysticism.

An interesting example of the symbolism in an image of the holy mountain is a Greek relief carving dating from the third century B.C., attributed to Archelaos, the son of Apollonius, a native of Priene (see figure 38 on page 136). It is believed to describe the apotheosis of Homer.[7] The carving is divided into four levels. At the lowest level may be seen an enactment of the sacred rites that open the entrance to the spiritual world, signified by the cave on the second level. It illustrates how through ritual purification and sacrifice the initiate enters the holy mountain to receive inspiration from the divine Godhead through the agency of one or more of the Muses.[8] At the summit reclines Zeus, the king of the gods.

In ancient Israel the sacred mount is Mt. Sinai, the mountain ascended by Moses. The biblical account of his ascent, which is given in Exodus, may be viewed as a veiled allegory concerning a system of mystical development whereby the soul may experience communion with God. Only a few (seventy elders[9]) were privy to its mysteries. This system of

---

6   *Ibid.*, p. 107.

7   A. B. Cook, *Zeus*, vol I (Cambridge: University Press, 1914), pp. 129–130.

8   Although there are variations of the theme, there are said to be nine Muses: Clio, the Muse of history; Euterpe, the Muse of flute playing; Thalia, the Muse of comedy; Melpomene, the Muse of tragedy; Terpsichore, the Muse of lyric poetry and dance; Erato, the Muse of love poetry; Polyhymnia, the Muse of meditation and mimic art; Urania, the Muse of astronomy; Calliope, the Muse of epic poetry and eloquence.

9   Exodus 24:1.

Fig. 38. Greek bas relief, third century B.C., thought to depict the apotheosis of Homer. From Arthur B. Cook, *Zeus* (Cambridge: Cambridge University Press, 1914).

ritualised prayer and meditation remained unchanged until the destruction of the first temple by the Babylonians.

During Israel's captivity in Babylon,[10] the teachings and visions of Ezekiel reformed the esoteric framework of the

---

[10] 585–538 B.C.

Mosaic system. In 538 B.C., Israel's captivity in Babylon came
to an end and the people of Israel were allowed to return to
Jerusalem and rebuild the Temple. Thus began the period of
the Second Temple. During this time an esoteric doctrine
evolved, derived from the first chapter of Ezekiel;[11] in it a
vision is described, a vision that became the basis of a system
of mystical development that gradually reformed the Mosaic
system. The primary objective of this system, known as
Merkabah Mysticism, is the experience of the throne-world
and the vision of God on his heavenly throne as described
by Ezekiel. In principle it is the same as the Mosaic system,
except that the objective of the ascent changed from communion with God to the ecstatic vision and experience of
the throne world. Indeed, many of the magical rituals that
emerged in the late medieval world had their origins in
Merkabah mysticism as defined by Ezekiel.

The word *Merkabah* means 'vehicle', a vehicle one can ride:
a chariot. Merkabah mysticism involves creating a vehicle
whereby an experience of the spiritual world may be attained.
Ezekiel's vision may be divided into two basic components:
the first describes the 'holy living creatures' who constitute
the basis of the chariot, and the second describes the 'Throne
of God' resting on or above the chariot. Upon the throne
sits God in the 'likeness of a man'. To become a 'rider of
the chariot', one must first create a chariot. The chariot is a
vehicle of light formed in the depths of meditation from the
spiritual material of one's prayers and devotion. The legend
of creating a golem—a magical homunculus created through
using a system of letter magic derived from the Sepher Yetzirah—is a medieval corruption of this concept.

The work of the Merkabah mystic requires a significant degree of competence in traditional meditation techniques,[12] and a precise and detailed knowledge of angelic

---

11   The 26th book of the Old Testament.

12   Concentration, relaxation, breath control, memory, and visualization.

names, seals, and qualities, without which the aspirant is doomed to failure and disappointment. It is also incumbent upon each aspirant to learn and to memorise a large amount of appropriate information because successful passage through the planetary realms and each one of the seven palaces requires the presentation of increasingly complex signs, seals, prayers, and invocations. To this end the Merkabah mystics of the Second Temple era developed a metaphysical system, subsequently described in the Sepher Yetzirah, that provides the basis for an algebraic language by which the mystic may engage in a technically precise and meaningful process of transcendental activity.

Preparation for the work involves frequent purification rites, constant prayer, and periods of fasting that might last as long as forty days. The work itself consists of an interior ascent through the seven planetary realms of the ancient world. In this ascent, the aspirant should be prepared to be confronted by astral and planetary entities and forces that will do their utmost to impede his or her progress. (Some historians believe this indicates Gnostic influence; however, the same influences may also be attributed to earlier Babylonian thought.)[13] Those who succeed in entering the seventh realm must then pass through the seven palaces or halls found therein.[14] At the entrance to each of these palaces the aspirant will be confronted by gatekeepers, or guardians, who will deny safe passage to the throne world unless the correct name, sign, and seal are produced. Having gained access to the throne world, the aspirant beholds the Throne of God and the sublime nature of the throne world.

---

[13] Stephen H. Langdon, *Semitic Mythology* in *The Mythology of all Races* vol. 5 (New York: Cooper Square, 1964), pp. 159–160; see also Arthur B. Cook, *Zeus: A Study in Ancient Religion* (Cambridge: University Press, 1914–1940), pp. 128–140.

[14] In the Diaspora, particularly in Alexandria, the exposure of the Jewish communities to the esoteric culture of the Greco-Roman world witnessed the introduction of the *Hekhaloth,* or 'Halls' to the Merkabah system. The concept of 'Halls', or 'Palaces', seems to have been unknown to Ezekiel.

The first stage of the ascent through the planetary spheres consists of rising above or transcending the sphere of the earth. The sphere of the earth is the physical body, and one must develop an understanding of the body's complex biology if one is to rise above it. This is because in this world the majority of our experience is defined by the chemistry of the body. Developing an understanding of the body's chemistry is not an easy matter as it is multifaceted and in a constant state of flux. However, through the observation and study of the complex nature of human biology one can attain an understanding of its chemistry, and thus be in a position to overcome the gravitational strength of the body. In short, it is possible to separate the chemist from the chemistry; and meditation is the ideal means by which this may be achieved.

In learning to rise above the mundane world of the body the methodology of the Pseudo-Dionysius is particularly useful; he teaches that one should first learn the ways of God through positive associations, meditating on the titles and names of God as given in Scripture. In *The Divine Names* he writes:

> But as for now, what happens is this. We employ appropriate symbols for things Divine; and then from these we press on upwards according to our powers to behold in simple unity the truth perceived by spiritual contemplations and leaving behind us all human notions of godlike things we still the activities of our minds and reach into the super-essential ray.[15]

This is in complete agreement with Kabbalistic doctrine. The reality is that the human mind is naturally dualistic and conditioned in the ways of the mundane world. It is only brought out of the hypnotic activities and influences of the mundane world, and then into a state of spiritual unity, by concentrating the will and the attention on a singular subject of a spiritual nature. Thus, meditating on the scriptures and

---

[15] C. E. Rolt, trans., *Dionysius the Areopagite on the Divine Names and The Mystical Theology* (Berwick, ME: Ibis Press, 2004), p. 58.

the divine names of God focuses the attention upon that which is spiritually essential, leading the mystic into a deeper understanding of the true nature of consciousness.

The Path of Names

Another method was favoured by the Kabbalist Abraham Abulafia, who in the thirteenth century developed a system of ecstatic or prophetic mysticism, which involved combining the letters of the Hebrew alphabet according to the rules of gematria, notarikon, and temurah (see chapter 3. pp. 83–86). Abulafia maintained that in its fall the soul was isolated from the mainstream of spiritual life by its identity with a Self formed in and by the mundane world. His teachings were directed toward enabling the soul to break all ties with the body and the mundane world. To achieve this he established a spiritual discipline designed to transcend the rational mind by overloading it with information of a spiritual nature. This spiritual discipline involved meditating first upon a complex system of combining Hebrew letters and their correspondences, then gradually narrowing one's focus to meditating upon the Tetragrammaton in all of its permutations. Abulafia's method drew heavily upon the Sepher Yetzirah. The following example is a good illustration:

> Twenty-two foundation letters: He engraved them, carved them, weighed them, and transposed them, Alef with them all. And He permuted them, and with them He formed the soul of all that was ever formed, and the soul of all that ever will be formed.[16]

By writing in a controlled and formal manner, with full attention concentrated upon the task in hand, the aspirant engraves the letters upon both the paper and the mind. In transferring

---

[16]   Aryeh Kaplan, *Sefer Yetzirah*, p. 273. Italics are my addition.

the attention from writing and shaping the letters, to think-ing and using the imagination to visualise each letter, with the same devoted attention, the aspirant *carves* the letters in the mind; and, by meditating, or thinking, about their significance, the aspirant *weighs* the letters. Then, by comparing, cross-refer-encing, and rearranging them they are *transposed* and *permuted* according to formulas passed in secret from teacher to student. Using this method it is possible to break the ties that bind the soul to the senses and the mind of the senses. Only then is it possible for the aspirant to establish a new state of conscious-ness, a state of consciousness pure enough to engage in the contemplation of the divine names of God according to the Tradition. This path is called the 'Path of Names'. His method broke away from the traditional method used by the Merkabah mystics, whose system was of a more theurgic nature.

THE CEASELESS PRAYER OF THE DESERT FATHERS

There are parallels between Abulafia's method and the medi-tation techniques developed during the third and fourth cen-turies A.D. by Christian monks in the desert communities of Egypt, Palestine, and Syria; indeed, the similarities suggest a direct connection or a common source of inspiration. Both preferred a life of seclusion and asceticism devoted to spiritual disciplines, and both used techniques designed to maintain prolonged periods of concentration. A key discipline of the Desert Fathers was the practise of ceaseless prayer, and in the desert communities many forms of ceaseless prayer were devel-oped, invariably consisting of short formulas that were often no more than a single word or name, and never more than a phrase or two. The value of such formulas rested in the fact that they may be used habitually, thereby becoming a natural and self-perpetuating reflex, which sublimates the incessant mental noise that is our common experience of the mundane world. This method is similar to Abulafia's technique of focusing the mind upon the letters of the alphabet, and systematically working with them in a spiritual context to the exclusion of all other sensory input. According to Abulafia, the art of combining letters within the context of controlled meditation is a 'mystical logic', which corresponds to the inner harmony of thought in its movement toward God.[17] Abulafia's system led from the vocal articulation of the permutation and combination of letters, to them being written down and contemplated. This method of *vocalization, writing* and *contemplation* constitutes a progressive and mystically logical system of pure meditation in which letters—the basis of each stage—manifest in increasingly spiritual forms, culminating in the sublime discipline of the 'Path of Names'.

In the desert communities the discipline of ceaseless prayer was set in the context of a secret language of the soul, a language that synthesises thought, image, and emotion into one thing, stepping as it were from the world of the senses to the interior domain of the heart wherein the realization of one's true nature is attained. This chemistry is underpinned by a method that enables the soul to transcend the limitation of the mundane world. This method describes four stages of prayer. The first is concerned with the repetitive vocalization of prayer; the second describes the methodical process of silently uttering and reflecting upon the nature and significance of the words uttered; the third is a less discursive engagement with the central theme of the words, wherein a more intuitive experience of spiritual reality may occur; the fourth and last is probably best described as a sublime form of agape, wherein the soul rests in the presence or light of God.

---

[17] Scholem, *Major Trends in Jewish Mysticism*, p. 134.

PATH WORKING

In recent times another method has emerged known as 'path working'. This is a modern term that describes a transcendental system of working with the Tree of Life. It is derived from methods used in Merkabah mysticism, but instead of the mantra-like uses of divine names, or the letter combinations used by Abulafia and his followers, the emphasis is given to meditating on images as visual gateways to specific astral or spiritual worlds. The images often used are the twenty-two tarot trumps. Each of the twenty-two trumps is attributed to a letter of the Hebrew alphabet and each letter to a specific pathway between the ten Sephiroth (see figure 31, p. 95 and Table 6, p. 97). Thus each tarot trump is understood to be a pictorial representation of the unique nature and quality of the path to which it is attributed. For example, in some systems the letter Beth is attributed to the path that lies between Kether and Binah, and the trump associated with it is the Magician.

The first person to attribute the tarot trumps to the Hebrew alphabet was the nineteenth century French occultist Alphonse Louis Constant, known as Éliphas Lévi, a deacon of the Roman Catholic church. In his book *Dogme et Rituel de la Haute Magie* (1856),[18] Lévi declared that the tarot generally, and the trumps in particular, were keys to understanding the mysteries of Kabbalah. He proposed that each of the twenty-two tarot trumps should be attributed to one of the twenty-two letters of the Hebrew alphabet.

Path working using the tarot trumps was first applied in a systematic way by members of the Hermetic Order of the Golden Dawn, a Christian and Rosicrucian Order devoted to the study of the Hermetic sciences. It is principally an act of controlled visualization, using the trump cards, or indeed any other pictorial image, as the focal point of one's attention. The image is to be visualised in the sphere of the imagination. The

---

[18] In the English speaking world, Lévi's book is better known in the translation by A. E. Waite, *Transcendental Magic: Its Doctrine and Ritual*.

technique requires the aspirant to use the same trump card every day for up to a month; eventually, the aspirant will know the image so well that the focus of attention will rest entirely upon the image in the sphere of the imagination. At a certain moment the aspirant will be able to enter the image, and to explore its environment, ranging further and further afield. It is a technique that requires a great deal of background knowledge and theoretical understanding; it also comes with a serious health and safety warning, for those who engage in such work without due preparation and guidance risk the health and integrity of their mind and soul.

The techniques underpinning path working remained within the domain and control of esoteric orders for some considerable time. However, from the mid-twentieth century onward it has become more widely known and used by many different organizations, ranging from off-shoot esoteric orders that have broken away from the founding Orders, to a wide range of neo-pagan and new-age organizations, many of which adapted the system as a basis for their meditations. Consequently, the basic concepts of path working have since been integrated with the quasi-meditative techniques of modern times to generate a whole range of guided fantasies. Such methods have little or no role to play in traditional Kabbalistic schools.

Path working, as understood in the schools, is an ascent— but not so much an ascent in time and space, astral or otherwise, but in consciousness—an ascent in understanding. At the beginning of the journey, the chemistry of consciousness is inevitably discursive and extremely reactive, and this must be brought under control. Thus, emblems and symbols were, and still are, used to draw the faculties of the mind to a single and central place. Behind every image and symbol is to be found an idea or principle, surrounded by a complex of associated meanings, and it is the understanding of such principles that is one of the main objectives. Moreover, when all of one's faculties are concentrated upon one object, then the chemistry of consciousness functions in a surprising manner, the imagination becomes charged by the attentive mind, which is to say that the combination of a mind absolutely focused, and engaging with a given subject or image, increases the power of imagination by an order of magnitude, to say the least, thereby generating many experiences, not only astral. However, this can be a trap for the unwary because such experiences, particularly of the astral world, can lead one into a hall of mirrors, a fleeting picture show that is more addictive than opium and just as delusory. The principal purpose of such a discipline as path working is to teach the student how to gather the faculties of the mind into one concentrated whole, from which an ascent in consciousness may begin. Emblems and symbols used as meditational aids in a method such as 'The Ladder' can be very effective in communicating profound truths that would be otherwise almost impossible to address. They can also be very useful tools for emancipating the image-making faculty—the imagination—from the instinctive nature and refining its powers, while furthering an understanding of some of the basic principles of the spiritual life.

RELAXATION TECHNIQUE FOR MEDITATION

Because relaxation is the first step toward becoming proficient in meditation it is important that you master the basic skills of relaxation, the key to which, especially at the beginning, lies in the regulation of the breath. Through the breath, you can establish effective control over the tensions within both your body and mind. It is indeed the fulcrum upon which effective meditation rests; hence the beginning of meditation is the beginning of a new attitude toward breathing.

Environment

- Allow yourself sufficient time free from commitments, to engage in this subject without haste.
- Wear loose, comfortable clothing.
- Chose a place that is clean and free from disturbance, i.e., people, telephones, noisy traffic, etc.
- Sit in a firm but comfortable chair, ensuring that your spine is straight and your head is balanced comfortably, without leaning too far forward or backward.
- Alternatively, lie down on the floor.

Breathing Exercise

The success of the relaxation technique outlined below depends upon gentle, rhythmic breathing. The method of rhythmic breathing is as follows:

- *Inhale* gently through your nostrils: your breath must be full but not strained
- *Hold* your breath for a moment
- *Exhale* gently through the nostrils, emptying the lungs completely
- *Hold* the breath for a moment
- Allow the breath to flow gently and easily—it will soon find its own level—force nothing.

One whole cycle includes: *inhale, hold, exhale, hold.*

Relaxation Exercise

1. Sit comfortably in a firm but comfortable chair, ensuring that your spine is straight and your head is balanced comfortably, without leaning too far forward or backward. Commence the above breathing exercise until your breath is flowing gently and easily.

2. Once established, focus your attention upon your *feet*, tense them, then relax them, and imagine all of the muscles of your feet loosening and becoming limp. Take your time, coordinate this, and all subsequent steps, with two or three cycles of the breathing exercise.

3. Focus your attention upon your *ankles*, tense them, then relax them, and imagine the muscles in your ankles loosening and becoming limp.

4. Focus your attention upon your *calves*, tense them, then relax them, and imagine the muscles in your calves loosening and becoming limp.

5. Focus your attention upon your *knees* and *thighs*, tense them, then relax them, and imagine the muscles in them loosening and becoming limp.

6. Focus your attention upon your *lower abdomen*, tense the muscles thereabouts, then relax them, and imagine all of the muscles therein loosening and becoming limp.

7. Focus your attention upon the muscles around your *solar plexus*, tense them, then relax them, and imagine all of these muscles loosening and becoming limp.

8. Focus your attention upon the muscles of your *back*, tense them, then relax them, and imagine them loosening and becoming limp.

9. Focus your attention upon the muscles of your *chest*, tense them, then relax them, and imagine all of them loosening and becoming limp.

10. Focus your attention upon the muscles of your *fingers* and *arms*, tense them, then relax them, and imagine all of them loosening and becoming limp.

11. Focus your attention upon the muscles of your *neck*, tense them, then relax them, and imagine all of the muscles of the neck loosening and becoming limp.

12. Focus your attention upon the muscles on and around your *head*, tense them, then relax them, and imagine them loosening and becoming limp.

13. Focus your attention upon the muscles around your *eyes*, tense them, then relax them, and imagine them loosening and becoming limp.

14. Focus your attention on the muscles of your *face* and *jaw*, tense them, then relax them and imagine them loosening and becoming limp.

15. Focus your attention on your *tongue*, tense it, then relax it, and imagine it loosening and becoming limp.

16. Now focus your attention upon your *whole body*, take note of how you feel and observe the influence that the ebb and flow of your breath has upon your overall condition. Allow the rhythm of your breathing to deepen the feeling of relaxation in your muscles.

Chapter 6

Magic

KABBALAH IS NOT a study of esoteric literature. We may read all of the spiritual and magical texts that have ever been written and still end up knowing nothing. Books, manuscripts, ancient scrolls and codices contain information, and information is only data; it gives neither wisdom nor understanding; it is not knowledge. If Kabbalah is a study at all, it is a study of the secret life of the soul in its relationship with God, the chemistry of which constitutes a secret doctrine. This may seem a strange statement to make, particularly as there is now so much written about it. Nevertheless, it remains a secret doctrine, and will ever remain so except to those who enter its sanctuaries, which are to be found within the secret garden of the soul. Words cannot adequately convey what it is, and pictures cannot portray the inner reality of that garden, and so Kabbalah will always remain a secret doctrine free from the crude speculations of a rational mind governed by the senses. To those who wish to explore Kabbalah as an intellectual exercise, wish them well, but know that they will not find the door that gives them access to its secrets. Indeed, there is no person or text on this earth that can give us that knowledge; we must find it within ourselves, and finding the doorway that leads into that inner garden is no easy task. It does not require intelligence so much as awareness, nor does it require goodness so much as a willingness to be led by goodness. No one is so base that they cannot enter; yet they cannot take their baseness with them. However, it does require a dedicated heart and a persevering will.

In the first chapter of this book I described the development of the tradition; it was a unique development, a spiritual impetus in the evolution of the soul of humanity that flowed out of an ancient civilisation through the Greco-Roman world into our own. In truth, if you were to seek, you would find the essence of Kabbalah in any of the world's great religions, but the Kabbalah as we know it emerged in the context of our cultural evolution, and doubtless it will continue to unfold as our culture changes. Arguably the greatest influence on the shape of Kabbalah was the Neoplatonic philosophy bequeathed to us by the classical world in its ember days, a philosophy that has in many ways flowed like an underground river through the mindscape of our emerging civilisation, acting as a catalyst to our nascent understanding, sometimes welcome, sometimes not. Today there are new opportunities facing the tradition as many people and movements challenge its teachings or claim it as their own. Fortunately the reality of Kabbalah is a spiritual reality, and it will adapt its outer form to suit the need of a new generation—the spiritual reality remains unchanged.

The basics of Kabbalah, as described throughout this book are tools for the soul to engage in the exploration of its own spiritual nature—an inner life that unfolds in the context of the Bible. The Bible is the heart of the Kabbalah, not the Bahir, not the Sepher Yetzirah, not even the Zohar—all Kabbalistic teachings concerning the inner life are set in a biblical context, and they are extremely subtle. Some people have strong prejudices against the Bible, a prejudice to be found even among those who have never read it. Many will have heard stories from it as children and still think of it as children, while for others, perhaps the violence, contradictions, and challenges to our modern thought make too great a handicap. Yet, it is a handicap worth overcoming, for everything a Kabbalist might need is to be found in the Bible. However, we must first learn to read it as adults, as something other than a book of fables. The earliest written version of the Bible was the Septuagint; it was the principal Bible used by both scholars and Kabbalists in the past. There are other versions—interlinear and parallel text Bibles—some of them are very useful, but be warned, the Bible does not give up its secrets easily.

One of the first tasks undertaken by a student is the development of a metaphysical language that enables the soul to operate at a much higher level than our everyday language generally allows. In part this begins with learning the Hebrew alphabet along with all of the correspondences that go with it. It is not so much a foreign language that needs to be learned as a mystical algebraic system, a system that is capable of many levels of permutation and interpretation.

Another task the student should undertake is to become acquainted with the cosmology on which the Kabbalah is based, as it will resolve many of the obscure issues that will arise along the way. Kabbalah is in part a modelling system that enables the soul to put into perspective the matrix of human consciousness, and to understand the dynamics of that consciousness. It is to this end that many Trees and maps are employed and directed.

Perhaps the most important task a student can undertake is to learn the art of meditation, which is a private and introspective process whereby in a state of deep relaxation the attention is concentrated upon a desired theme. Consequently, anyone seeking to become proficient in meditation must acquire two basic skills: first, in relaxation, because effective meditation requires a stable biological platform; and second, in concentration, because it is through concentration that we overcome the transient activities of our mind. Most traditional methods of meditating are based on the premise that the discursive activities of the mind can be brought to a standstill by focusing the attention on one subject to the exclusion of all others. In some systems it is the breath, in others it is a word or a phrase that is the focal point. In all instance, extraneous thoughts and sensations will make a nuisance of themselves. Many people find when they first begin meditation, they either become very uncomfortable physically or their minds become very active, more active than normal, bringing the endeavour to a frustrating halt. For most of us this is a common experience and we should not let it put us off. The antidote to such interference is persistence and the strength of one's intention.

With regard to the subject matter of Kabbalah, it is so immense that an in-depth exploration of the material it encompasses could never be addressed in a single volume such as this, which has been designed simply to introduce the reader to some of the fundamental building blocks of this complex, multilayered system of spiritual development. There is a great deal of material that we have not touched upon at all, and there are subjects that we have touched upon, but only just. One of these is 'Practical Kabbalah', which many today believe deals with ceremonial and talismanic magic and related disciplines. However, magic and Practical Kabbalah do not necessarily mean the same thing to a traditional student of the Kabbalah as they do to the majority of aspiring magicians. Indeed, strictly speaking, in the traditional schools there is no such thing as magic: to the Kabbalist, Practical Kabbalah is an exercise in practical mysticism rather than an exercise in magic. This distinction

is important, because to the Kabbalist the central teachings
of Kabbalah are the scriptures, and therein many aspects of
what we call magic are forbidden, for example, 'There shall
not be found among you anyone who practises witchcraft,
or a soothsayer, or one who interprets omens or a sorcerer
or one who conjures spells, or a medium or a spiritist or one
who calls up the dead. For all who do these things are an
abomination to the Lord'.[1] Not a popular text in the modern
world, yet many traditional Kabbalists would denounce the
common understanding of Practical Kabbalah on the basis
of this passage alone.

In some respects the term 'Practical Kabbalah' is misleading for it implies that in Kabbalah there are separate
departments. But this is simply not the case as all Kabbalah is practical in its own way. Indeed, one would do well
to remember that the divisions described in chapter two
are arbitrary divisions devised by authors to rationalise the
complex material of Kabbalah, much of which, since the late
middle ages, has been appropriated by enterprising magicians and adapted to serve their own purposes. A lot of this
material is claimed to be 'pure Kabbalah', but in reality has
little connection with it, or any understanding of its traditions. Furthermore, a great deal of material from the late
medieval period onward, which has been classified under
the heading of 'Practical Kabbalah', derives from non-
Kabbalistic sources. For example, most of the material from
the work of the sixteenth-century magicians John Dee and
Edward Kelly, has little to do with Kabbalah, practical or
otherwise.

Over the course of the last century Practical Kabbalah has
attracted the attention of so many aspiring magicians that
today the words 'Kabbalah' and 'Magic' have become synonymous. It may then be pertinent at this point to ask the
question, what is magic, what does the word actually mean?

---

[1] Deuteronomy 18:10–12.

The simple answer is that the word 'Magic' has meant, and continues to mean, many things to many people. There is nothing new in this; it has been the subject of a great deal of debate over the centuries and there is as yet no consensus as to its meaning; in fact the meaning of the word has been a matter of uncertainty since classical times.[2] What is known is that the word Magic is generally accepted as being derived from the Greek *mageia* (μαγεια), a word that the Greeks derived from the word 'Magu' or 'Magi', a title of the sacerdotal caste of ancient Persia and Media, who were followers of the prophet Zoroaster and priests of the god Ahuramazda. The word 'Magi' signifies those who are wise, not only in the ways of the world, but also in the ways of God, and because of their wisdom the Magi commanded great respect throughout the ancient world. Plato, when discussing statesmanship in *Alcibiades I*, felt comfortable using them as exemplars of the highest virtue. He describes how a royal prince of ancient Persia, upon reaching the age of fourteen years, was put in the care of four carefully selected masters (magians). These masters were 'reputed to be the best among the Persians of a certain age; and one of them is the wisest, another the most just, the third the most temperate, and the fourth the most valiant. The first instructs him in the magianism of Zoroaster, the son of Ahuramazda, which is the worship of the gods, and teaches him also the duties of his royal office . . '.[3] Thus Plato held the Magi in the highest esteem, and furthermore, informs us that the work of a magus, or magician, is the worship of the gods (theurgy). The classical world came to an end with the collapse of the Western Roman Empire in the fifth century, to be followed by the Dark Ages and the medieval era, throughout which magic generally fell under three main headings: natural magic, goetia, and theurgy.

---

[2]   Lynn Thorndike, *A History of Magic and Experimental Science*, vol. 1 (New York: Macmillan, 1923), p. 4.

[3] B. Jowett, trans., *The Dialogues of Plato*, vol. I (Oxford: Clarendon Press, 1953), p. 654.

Natural Magic

Natural magic is concerned with the hidden workings of nature—its properties, powers, qualities, substances, and virtues. Natural magic was held to the noblest part of the physical sciences, and as such was not forbidden by faith and was therefore not legislated against. For many students of the magical art it was the consummation of natural philosophy. The study of alchemy, medicine, astrology, and the manipulation of nature's 'finer forces' were considered to be the proper domain of natural magic. One of the greatest exponents of natural magic was Paracelsus, a renowned healer of the sixteenth century who became famous for his Doctrine of Signatures, in which he proposed that natural objects suggest by their external appearance the complaints for which they were cures; thus, some plants may be seen as representing parts of the body, while others suggest diseases for which they may be used as remedies. A 'signature' was therefore any distinctive feature or quality that indicated a connection between remedy and malady.

Natural magic was understood to be the application of true and natural causes to produce rare and unusual effects by means that were neither superstitious nor diabolical. It follows then, that there is a fundamental distinction between the field of natural magic and those of goetia and theurgy, for natural magic does not involve engaging with spirits or gods, be they good or bad. Rather, it is a discipline of inquiring into the workings of nature, whereas goetia and theurgy are generally considered to be magical disciplines that do engage with spirits and gods—and indeed, with a vast hierarchy of other supernatural beings.

GOETIA

To the ancient Greeks, what we in our time might generally understand by the terms sorcerer, witch, and witchcraft was known by the name *Goēs* or *Goētes*, from which the term goetia and goetic are derived. Indeed, from the earliest times the term goetia has been employed in a sinister and disreputable sense. Goetia has invariably been linked with magical ceremonies devised to control and manipulate spirits for questionable reasons, often to the detriment of others. Today goetia is usually associated with the seventeenth century grimoire, *Lemegeton Clavicula Solomonis*, otherwise known as *The Lesser Key of Solomon*, around which a vast amount of fanciful myth and legend has accumulated. Indeed, goetia has long been considered to be synonymous with 'black magic'. Historically, Goēs (sorcerers, witches, etc.) were often seen as a threat to the social order and there were occasions when the laws against them were vigorously enforced, particularly in the Roman Empire. Almost from the beginning, Rome introduced laws against the exponents of sorcery and witchcraft. The earliest Roman code of law, the 'Twelve Tablets',—introduced in the mid-fifth century B.C., and so named because they were publicly displayed in the Forum on twelve tablets of bronze—forbade people from using magic to harm others, the punishment for such a crime being severe. In the first century B.C. the patrician Felix Lucius Cornelius Sulla, reformed these laws, part of which, the *Lex Cornelia de sicariis et veneficis* (*The Cornelian Law Concerning Assassins and Poisoners*), includes the following statements with regard to magic:

> Persons who celebrate, or cause to be celebrated impious or nocturnal rites, so as to enchant, bewitch, or bind anyone, shall be crucified, or thrown to wild beasts.

> Persons who are addicted to the art of magic, shall
> suffer extreme punishment; that is to say they shall be
> thrown to wild beasts, or crucified. Magicians them-
> selves shall be burned alive.
>
> No one shall be permitted to have books on the art
> of magic in his possession, and when they are found
> with anyone, they shall be publicly burnt, and those
> who have them, after being deprived of their property,
> if they are of superior rank shall be deported to an
> island, and if they are of inferior station shall be put to
> death; for not only is the practice of this art prohib-
> ited, but also the knowledge of the same.[4]

Obviously, the ancient world was no bed of spiritual roses, for society then, just like today, had its share of unscrupulous people who were prepared to use both natural and supernatural forces to take advantage of and/or intimidate their neighbours. However, in Plato or Sulla's time it would have been unlikely that a sorcerer or witch would have been mistaken for being a member of the Magi, for the Magi, whether from Persia, ancient Egypt, Greece, or Rome, were the elite of their civilisation. They were extremely learned, not only in spiritual sciences such as theology and psychology, but in all of the known empirical sciences, including astronomy, mathematics, metallurgy, philosophy, medicine, and physiology, and as such were highly respected. As Plato so eloquently put it, the work of the Magi was *the worship of the gods*; work that is formally known as theurgy.

Theurgy

The word 'theurgy' is based upon the Greek words *Theos* (God) and *Ergos* (work), from which is derived the word *theourgia*, which means 'works of God' or 'divine workings'.[5] These divine workings were the sacramental rites or myster-

4   *Sentences of Paulus* 5.23: 15–18. See Stephen Benko, *Pagan Rome and the Early Christians* (London: Batsford, 1985), p. 128–129.

5   H. G. Liddell and R. Scott, *Greek – English Lexicon* (Oxford: Clarendon Press, 1883).

ies that were central to the spiritual life of the ancient world. One of the main exponents of theurgy in the ancient world was Iamblichus, who was born in Syria in the middle of the third century. He was the author of several books, most of which are now lost. Fortunately one book, *De Mysteriis*, survived. It is an account of a lengthy correspondence about Theurgy between an Egyptian high priest called Abammon, and Iamblichus's teacher, Porphyry. [6] It is perhaps the most significant work concerning ancient theurgic principles and dynamics still in existence.

Over the course of time the principles and dynamics of theurgy were absorbed into the sacramental system of the expanding Church, enriching and ennobling the ceremonial life therein. However, over the last century or so they have gradually fallen into disuse, being no longer valued or understood. Indeed, our society has barely any knowledge of the sacred rites of spiritual regeneration that were so important to the ancient world. This is hardly surprising as the secular world today views the spiritual dimension of life as a potpourri of primitive beliefs, practises, and superstitions promoted by the unscrupulous with the intention of fleecing the naïve and the incredulous, or by the misguided and the irrational as a delusory mystical science that rests more on hopes, dreams, and misconceptions than on any objective truth or observation. Even the majority of those who are knowledgeable perceive theurgy and goetia to be by and large one and the same thing. Unfortunately it is a potentially hazardous perception as the objectives and dynamics of theurgy and goetia are very different: on their own terms they are diametrically opposed. Éliphas Lévi says of goetic magic, 'This torrent of universal life . . . it is this which brings to our evocations and to the conjurations of our Goëtic Magic such swarms of

---

6 Porphyry (A.D. 232–305): The best known disciple of Plotinus. It was he who undertook the difficult task of editing the lecture notes and essays of Plotinus, and published them under the title of the *Enneads*, and for which we shall ever be in his debt, particularly for Plotinus' biographical details that he thoughtfully included in the Introduction.

larvæ and phantoms. Therein are preserved all the fantastic and fortuitous assemblages of forms which people our nightmares with such abominable monstrosities'.[7] Herein we may perceive the distinction between goetia and theurgy, for in goetia the magician seeks to control the forces of nature and the spirits that abound in creation, to take heaven by storm, to become as a god; 'Let my will be done' is the rule, whereas the theurgist seeks purification, liberation, and salvation of the soul, following a path of 'Thy will be done' as opposed to 'My will be done'. This is best summed up by Iamblichus himself, who wrote:

> From the beginning, it is necessary to divide ecstasy into two species: one is turned towards the inferior, filled with foolishness and delirium, but the other imparts goods more honourable than human wisdom.
>   The former is unstable, the latter unchangeable; the first is counter to nature, the latter is beyond nature; the former makes the soul descend, the latter raises it up; and while the former entirely separates the soul from participation in the divine, the latter connects the soul with the divine.[8]

From the foregoing it becomes obvious that describing what is meant by 'magic' is at best a little tricky. As mentioned above, magic has meant different things to different people at different times, but, if there is a common theme that runs throughout the history of magic, it is control. In all systems of magic throughout history, people have sought to control by magical means both their material and spiritual environment, and all things in it. In material terms many in today's world see all magic as a delusory pseudo-science, and so it

---

[7]   Eliphas Levi, *Transcendental Magic*, A. E. Waite, trans. (London: Rider & Co., 1923), p. 95.

[8]   As translated by Gregory Shaw in *Theurgy and the Soul* (Pennsylvania: Pennsylvania State University, 1995) p. 235. Otherwise see Thomas Taylor, *Iamblichus on The Mysteries*, Book 3, chapter XXV.

might be, but in spiritual terms magic is also a term for the inevitable technology that emerges from theology.

However, as we have seen, there is magic and there is magic. Broadly speaking, natural magic, traditionally concerned with exploring and controlling the natural world, has over the course of time naturally evolved into the sciences. The other systems of magic are generally understood to fall either under the banner of 'divine workings', which is known as theurgy, or under the banner of the 'diabolical', which is known as goetia. Although, it is a matter of some debate as to whether theurgy should be described as magic at all.

Historically, it would appear that magic has consistently been regarded with suspicion, but in the schools of Kabbalah the 'divine workings' have never been considered to be magic. As stated earlier, the Kabbalist is neither a magician nor seeks to become a magician. It may be difficult for an impartial observer to grasp the significance of this point, but it will become clear if one understands that to the Kabbalist, Practical Kabbalah is concerned only with the divine names of God as derived from Scripture and their mysterious workings as unfolded in Kabbalistic processes. The divine names are intimately connected with the Sephirotic world and its emanation, thus, to engage with the divine names is to engage in a sacred process, not a magical process. To the Kabbalist, such processes are geared only to the regeneration of the soul, not to its elevation, aggrandisement, or for its intellectual curiosity. From the time of the Sepher Yetzirah, and probably before, a complex and sophisticated system evolved concerning the application and use of the divine names in the art of spiritual regeneration. For the Kabbalist this system constitutes the essence of Practical Kabbalah. However, in the late Middle Ages, this system passed into the realms of ceremonial magic from which a degraded form of Practical Kabbalah emerged, and many scholars and magicians have never really seen the two as separate entities. Concerning this, A. E. Waite states that:

> The White and Black Magic of the Middle Ages constitutes a kind of spurious practical Kabbalah which represents Jewish esoteric doctrine debased to the purposes of the sorcerer, and it is necessary that we should estimate it at its true worth, because it has been the subject of misconception not only among uninstructed persons but even professed expositors.
>
> A study of Zoharistic writings, their developments and commentaries will shew the ends proposed by the Speculative Kabbalah are very different from evocations of spirits, the raising of ghosts, discovery of concealed treasures, the bewitchments and other mummeries of Ceremonial Magic. The Kabbalah does, however, countenance, as we have seen, the doctrine of a power resident in Divine Names, and it is in fact one of the burdens of its inheritance.[9]

The study of Kabbalah is no lightweight undertaking. Although its outer skin—by which I mean the glyphs of the Tree of Life, the four worlds, and the alphabet, and their correspondences—may serve well even the most casual dabbler in esoteric workings, it is not a path suited to those with a casual interest or dilettante attitude. It is, after all is said and done, a central part of the mysteries most suited to those souls whose love of the spirit is greater than their love of the world. Indeed, its inner sanctuaries are only accessible to those who are brave enough to give up the world, to leave the herd, as it were, for things divine are not attainable by those who comprehend the body alone, but only by those who, 'Stripped of their garments arrive at the summit'.[10] Such is the way of Kabbalah.

To be 'stripped' of our garments requires that we must first identify them for what they are—bodies that we wear like layers of clothing. Different authors have described them in different

---

9   Waite, *The Holy Kabbalah*, pp. 518-519.

10 Westcott, *Chaldean Oracles*, in *Collectanea Hermetica*, Oracle 169.

ways, some speak of them as etheric and astral bodies, others refer to them as subtle bodies, many refer to them as sheaths or vehicles. All of them allude to an understanding that the human vehicle we call a body consists not only of many different systems such as the arterial, digestive, and nervous systems, but also several unique elements or bodies that are incorporated within and about the physical frame. Each body is recognised as being of a different density and frequency of vibration. Thus one model proposes a physical body, an electromagnetic body, and a body of light each contained within the other—the physical within the etheric and the etheric within the body of light. There are many models and definitions concerning the nature and arrangement of these bodies, but it matters little what they are called, whether they be sheaths, bodies, vehicles, or indeed garments, they all amount to the same thing in the end: fields of human experience.

To identify these 'garments' is an important step in the work of a Kabbalist, not simply to know that they exist and give them labels, but to actually perceive them for what they are and what they do, to have direct knowledge of them. However, the work of identification is a slow process: it is more a growth in understanding than a noting of a specific object or event. To perceive the activities of the etheric is to see the Nephesh in action, but it is not with the eyes that this thing is perceived, but with the inner eye of an attentive and reflective mind. What follows is a frequently uncomfortable but necessary education as the soul slowly modifies its conduct, and consequently the nature of the Nephesh. In the schools this education comes under the heading of the 'civic virtues', which are courage, justice, temperance, and prudence, all of which may be found in the tarot trumps.

Courage refers to the student's ability to control and educate that part of the soul that is subject to anger. It requires bravery and non-attachment as we learn to walk away from the herd and establish our own values. This requires time because such qualities grow out of experience. Justice consists in understanding the nature and value of duty and in ordering our life so that we may live in harmony with our fellows. Temperance means controlling the appetitive nature, which at the beginning is driven by instinct and full of self-interest. Temperance teaches us to harmonise appetite and reason so that we may transcend the animal nature and become fit for greater things. Prudence is the manifestation of the rational part of the soul, which functions at its best when it is not serving the needs and demands of the animal nature. Thus, prudence requires that we learn to manage our existence according to reason governed by a spiritual philosophy, because without such a philosophy we will never be free of the mundane world.

In developing our nature, in cultivating and refining it so that it may serve the highest purpose we can envisage, we grow in spirit and slowly shed the influences of the 'garments' that we have worn throughout our lives. In Kabbalistic terms, the student who has mastered the Nephesh and cared for it with kindness is given entrance to the house of the Ruach, whose powers transform the civic virtues into a powerhouse of catharsis. Within the illuminating presence of the Ruach the student begins a new life, a life that is no longer rooted in the darkness of complete ignorance, but a life that increases in knowledge as it grows in the presence of the divine. In this blessed state the soul comes of age. It remains to be said that all that has been written in this book concerning Kabbalah is directed toward helping you find that place.

Appendix A

People and Places

Ashkenazim. One of the two main divisions of the Diaspora (the other being Sephardim). The word comes from the Hebrew, *Ashkenaz*, which means 'people of the north'. Originally the term was applied only to Jews living in Germany, but as time went by it also referred to the Jews of Northern France and Eastern Europe, particularly Poland and Russia. The Ashkenazim are distinguished from the Sephardim, the Jews of Spain, Portugal, and Mediterranean countries in general, by their liturgical practise and the pronunciation of Hebrew. Until the twentieth century, Yiddish was widely spoken by the Ashkenazim, from whom most American Jews are descended.

Azriel of Gerona (*ca.* 1160–1238). Azriel was a disciple of Isaac the Blind and one of the leading members of the Gerona school. He is recognised as being one of the greatest thinkers in Kabbalistic mysticism. He wrote commentaries on the ten Sephiroth, the Sefer Yetzirah, and several treatises on mysticism. His work clearly demonstrates the influence of Neoplatonism upon medieval Kabbalistic thought. Azriel is not to be confused with his older contemporary, Ezra ben Solomon, who was not only a member of the same school but was also known as Azriel.

Abraham Abulafia (1240– *ca.* 1291). Abulafia was born in Saragossa, Spain, in A.D. 1240. He developed a system of ecstatic or prophetic mysticism that involved combining the letters of the Hebrew alphabet according to the rules of gematria, notarikon, and temurah. He differed from the main current of thirteenth-century Spanish Kabbalistic exegesis, which was essentially symbolic, in that his system was geared towards inducing psycho-dynamic changes more in line with the ecstatic mysticism of Ashkenazic Hasidism. In this respect he was undoubtedly influenced by the Kabbalah of Eleazer of Worms. He favoured the isolationism that was more in keeping with hermits and Hesychasts, indeed, his methods were not so far removed from the techniques developed by the Desert Fathers in the third and fourth centuries.

Abulafia, like many ecstatic Kabbalists, wandered from place to place attracting disciples. In this he was relatively successful; but he also attracted many enemies. At one point he approached Pope Nicholas III with the intention of reprimanding him about the persecution of Jews. He was thrown into prison and sentenced to death. However, the pope died and the execution was cancelled. Abulafia's personal mystical experiences induced in him messianic pretensions and he was persecuted by his fellow Jews far more than by the Christian church. He was driven from Sicily in the mid-1280s and forced to go into exile on the Maltese island of Comino. The conflict with the congregation on Sicily continued in the form of a polemic between Abulafia and Ibn Adret, a Kabbalist and Halakhic scholar until Abulafia's death sometime after 1291.

Moses ben Jacob Cordovero (*ca.* 1522–1570). Cordovero was the most important Kabbalist in Safed and was recognised as the principal master of esoteric studies in Kabbalah, although he himself thought of Karo as his master. Cordovero is the author of several influential works—the *Pardes Rimmonim* (*Garden of Pomegranates*); the *Tomer Devorah* (*The Palm Tree of Deborah*); and the '*Or Yagar* (*The Precious Light*) being the best known of them. His disciples included most of the great Kabbalists of Safed; Abraham Galante, Abraham ben Eliezer ha-Levi Berukhim, Elijah de Vidas, Hayyim Vital, Eleazar Azikri, Samuel Gallico, and Isaac Luria. His life's work was an endeavour to synthesise the different trends of Kabbalah into a unified system. Cordovero was succeeded by Isaac Luria.

Eleazar of Worms (*ca.* 1165– *ca.* 1230). Eleazar ben Judah of Worms was the last major exponent of the Haside Ashkenaz movement in Germany. Eleazar was a member of the Kalonymus family; he was born in Mainz sometime around 1165. Although he travelled and studied in many centres of learning in France and Germany, he spent most of his life in Worms. Eleazar witnessed his wife and children being murdered by soldiers in one of the Crusader persecutions of Jews that were taking place in the late twelfth and early thirteenth centuries. His major mystical work is *Sodei Razayya* (*Secrets of Secrets*). The first part deals with a study of creation based upon the letter symbolism of the Sepher Yetzirah; the second part deals with the secrets of the angels, the holy throne, the Chariot, and prophecy; the third part is devoted to an exposition of the names of God explaining the methods that were used by the Hasidim; the fourth part is concerned with the psychology of the soul, the posthumous state of the soul, and the meaning of dreams; the fifth and final part of this work was a commentary on the Sepher Yetzirah. Eleazar became a legendary figure who was believed to be the custodian of the secret lore of Kabbalah. He was also thought to travel from place to place on a cloud. His best known disciples were Azriel and Isaac of Vienna, neither of whom was able to continue his work after he died.

Marsilio Ficino (1433–1499). Priest, philosopher, physician, humanist, and poet, Ficino was born in 1433, the son of Cosimo Medici's physician. From an early age he was nurtured by Cosimo Medici, who saw the brilliant potential in the young Ficino, and while still relatively young he was asked by Medici to lead the Florentine Platonic Academy, which he did with great energy and vision. Ficino translated, for the first time, Plato's complete works into Latin. Among his extraordinary achievements were his translations of Plotinus, Hesiod, Porphyry, Proclus, Iamblichus, Alcinous, Synesius, Psellus, Pythagoras, and the works of Dionysius the Areopagite. Through Ficino, Lorenzo the Magnificent—Cosimo Medici's successor—was able to introduce artists such as Botticelli, Michelangelo, and Leonardo da Vinci, and philosophers such as Pico della Mirandola and Reuchlin, to the sublime realms of Platonic and Hermetic thought, and through the Platonic Academy to influence in many ways the unfolding of the Renaissance throughout Europe.

Dion Fortune (1890–1946). Dion Fortune, was the pseudonym inspired by her family motto '*Deo, non fortuna*'

(God, not fate), of Violet Mary Firth, who was born at Llandudno, Wales. Her first magical mentor was Theodore Moriarty. In 1919 she was initiated into the Golden Dawn, at the London Temple of the Alpha et Omega, before transferring to the Stella Matutina. In 1922 she left the order and formed the Society of the Inner Light, which remained the focal point of her work for the rest of her life. She wrote several novels and short stories that explored aspects of magic and mysticism. The titles include *The Demon Lover*, *The Winged Bull*, *The Goat-Foot God*, and *The Secrets of Dr. Taverner*, this latter book being a collection of short stories based on her experiences with Theodore Moriarty. She also wrote several nonfiction books, the most significant being *The Mystical Qabalah* (1935), which is an introduction to the Kabbalah, and *Psychic Self-Defence*, which is a manual on how to protect oneself from psychic attacks.

Adolphe Franck (1809–1893). Adolphe Franck was a renowned French philosopher, Hebraist, and Orientalist. His family had earmarked him for a career as a rabbi, and to that end he was put under the care and tutelage of Marchand Ennery. However, he found his true vocation in philosophy and developed a successful career in that field, teaching at the colleges of Douai, Nancy, Versailles, and at the Collège Charlemagne in Paris. In 1844 he was elected to the French Academie des Sciences Morales et Politiques, and in 1856 he became professor of natural and civil law at the Collège de France; a position he held for thirty years. He wrote many books, including *La Kabbale ou Philosophie Religieuse des Hebreux*, which was published in Paris 1843, and reprinted 1899. In this book, Franck traces the beginnings of the

Kabbalah to the ancient Zoroastrians, and explores in some detail the evolution of the doctrine of the Kabbalah as expressed in the Sepher Yetzirah and the Zohar. It was first translated into English by I. Sossnitz and published in New York, 1926 and republished by University Books in 1967.

School of Gerona. Under the influence of the Provençal Kabbalists, the teachings of the Kabbalah spread to Spain, where they found a welcoming response in the rabbinic circles of Gerona, an ancient city of Catalonia in northeast Spain. An important Jewish community existed there from the eleventh century until the expulsion of the Jews from Spain in 1492. This school was active throughout the first half of the thirteenth century and was the most important and influential catalyst in the development of Kabbalistic thought of its time. The leading figures of this school were Moses ben Nahmanides, Azriel, and Ezra ben Solomon (also known as Azriel). Of this school Gershom Scholem writes, 'In the history of the old Kabbalah, therefore, this [School of Gerona] was a group of epoch moment. It stepped into the light of the history of religions undisguised and in full force. This group was composed of direct and indirect disciples of Isaac the Blind'.[1]

Joseph ben Abraham Gikatilla (1248–ca.1325). Gikatilla was a Spanish Kabbalist who was born in the region of Medinaceli, Castile. His influence as a Kabbalist has been significant and long-lasting. In his day, he provided a comprehensive and methodical exposition of Kabbalah as well as being the main proponent of the doctrine equating En-Sof with the first of the ten Sephiroth. Between 1272 and 1274, he studied under Abraham Abulafiah, who praised him

---

[1]   Gershom Scholem, *Origins of the Kabbalah*, p. 366-67.

as his most successful student. Gikatilla was deeply influenced by Abulafia's ecstatic Kabbalah, and probably as a result of this influence wrote a book in 1274, titled *Ginnat Egoz*, as an introduction to the mystical symbolism of the alphabet and vowel points. He was to write several treatises on the mystical significance of letters and their combination. At some point after 1280, Gikatilla came into contact with the author of the Sefer ha-Zohar, Moses ben Shem Tov de Leon. The influence flowed both ways, Gikatilla expounding the letter mysticism of Abulafiah and de Leon expounding the doctrines embodied in the Zohar. Gikatilla's most influential work, the *Sha'arei Orah* (*Gates of Light*), was probably written in response to this fertile relationship. It contains a detailed explanation of Kabbalistic symbolism and the ten Sephiroth from the perspective of the school of Gerona and the Zohar.

Christian Ginsburg (1831–1914). Christian David Ginsburg was born in Warsaw of Jewish parents. In 1846 he converted to Christianity, and shortly after moved to England. He was a renowned Bible scholar who devoted his life to the study of Scripture, particularly Masoretic texts of the Bible. His magnum opus, *The Massorah*, in which Ginsburg drew together a mass of rare and valuable material, was published in four volumes between 1880 and 1905. In 1865 his book *The Kabbalah, Its Doctrines, Development and Literature*, was published. It was for many years the most informative book on Kabbalah available in English; and it is still a very useful text for serious students.

Haside Ashkenaz. This medieval religious movement emerged in Germany in the mid-twelfth century. The first centres were in the Jewish communities of

Regensburg, Speyer, Worms, and Mainz; from where it spread throughout Germany and parts of France. As a movement it was undoubtedly influenced by Neoplatonic thought, but its main influence came from an esoteric tradition that had been maintained by the Kalonymus family[2] who, it is said, received it from one of the Carolingian emperors in the ninth century. This movement was a development away from the Merkabah (Chariot) mysticism, which had dominated Jewish esoteric thought for so many centuries, toward the magical disciplines of evocative prayer. These disciplines readily opened the doors to the psychic world, and to the few, the contemplation of the mysteries of the Godhead and the realm of archetypes.

Its central figures included Samuel ben Kalonymus he-Hasid, his son Judah ben Kalonymus he-Hasid, and Eleazar ben Judah b. Kalonymus of Worms. The teachings of these mystics are collected in the *Sepher Hasidim* (The Book of the Devout). In keeping with contemporary Christian mysticism they advocated a disciplined life of prayer and asceticism, fostering the virtue of humility to the extent of rejecting honours and accepting insults. Moral judgements were based upon ethical considerations rather than Talmudic teachings. The Haside Ashkenaz are not to be confused with the Eastern European eighteenth-century movement in known as Hasidism.

Hasidism. A popular religious movement founded in the eighteenth century by Rabbi Israel ben Eliezer, who was otherwise known as the *Baal Shem-Tov*.[3] This movement began in the regions of Volhynia and

---

[2] Kalonymus family: A notable Jewish family living in Germany which flourished in the early Middle Ages. Its members played a significant role in the religious and philosophical life of European Judaism.

[3] Master of the Holy Name.

Podolia, situated in the Sabbatian[4] heartlands of the Carpathian mountains. His teachings were the antithesis of the barren scholasticism of his contemporaries. He rejected the Talmud and taught that all are equal before God, and that purity of heart is superior to study. Prayer and the joyful obedience to God's commandments was the essence of his teaching, as God, who is present in all things, is open to all who are prepared to approach him. Those who are able to give themselves totally to God become the beloved of God—a zaddik, (perfected one). The zaddik is one who has found union with God, and was understood to be gifted with miraculous powers of healing and prophecy. Deeply influenced by the Kabbalah of Isaac Luria, the Hasid accepted the spiritual ideal of joyfulness in the service of God, and engaged in mystical and contemplative prayer through which he believed it possible to achieve union with the divine. However, one of the principal teachings of Hasidism also calls for the worship of God through physical acts such as eating, working, and sexual relations. In this way it is possible to redeem the divine sparks imprisoned in matter. The teachings of Hasidim were transmitted through meetings that were organised as prayer circles, around which Hasidic communities were established.

The Baal Shem was succeeded by Rabbi Baer of Meseritz, who systemised Hasidic teaching. Although the Hasidim were bitterly opposed by the Talmudists, the movement spread throughout Eastern Europe and beyond. Unfortunately, the great centres of Hasidism were wiped out during World

---

4   Sabbatians: Followers of the pseudo-messiah, Shabbetai Tzevi, a Turkish scholar and Kabbalist of the seventeenth century. He later converted to Islam to save himself from being executed by the sultan at Constantinople.

War II, although several family lines did establish themselves in the U.S.A., where the movement continues to exert an important influence on Judaism.

Rabbi Isaac the Blind (*ca.* 1160–1235). Son of Rabbi Abraham ben David of Posqueres (Spain). Little is known of Isaac the Blind's life other than the anecdotes and traditions preserved among his disciples. He has been called the 'father of the Kabbalah'. His teachings consolidated many of the mystical speculations of his day into a working system that was to become central to Kabbalah for centuries to follow. He developed a system of contemplative mysticism that led to spiritual union through meditation on the Sephiroth, which he taught were stages of the hidden life of God. He was a key figure in Kabbalistic circles of both Provence and Spain. His teachings were mainly transmitted through the Kabbalah School of Gerona, a small town lying between the Pyrenees and Barcelona. He was once believed to be the author of the Sepher ha Bahir.

Aryeh Kaplan (1934–1983). Rabbi Aryeh Kaplan was born in the Bronx, New York City. After his ordination in Jerusalem, he earned a master's degree in physics, and was able to demonstrate in his writings a masterful balance of science and theology. In his short life he became one of the most significant exponents of Jewish mysticism and Kabbalah of the late twentieth century. He produced more than fifty books on a wide range of spiritual topics, including prayer, marriage, and meditation. He translated many books into English, including *The Living Torah*, a notable and scholarly translation of the Pentateuch. His translations of the Sepher Ha-Bahir and the Sepher Yetzirah are both still very useful and in print.

Rabbi Joseph ben Ephriam Karo (1488–1575). Karo was one
of the greatest Jewish legal luminaries, author of the
Beit Yosef, a commentary on Jacob ben Asher's *Arbaah
Turim,* and the *Shulhan Arukh,* a standard code of
Jewish law. Karo was born in Toledo, but after the
expulsion from Spain in 1492 he moved to Turkey
where he remained for about forty years. In 1536 he
left Turkey for Safed where he became the head of a
large academy. In Safed, Karo became a member of
a school of mystics that included Moses Cordovero,
Solomon Alkabetz, and Isaac Luria. Karo was understood to be the beneficiary of a spiritual mentor
known among Kabbalists as a *maggid.* Karo's maggid
revealed itself to him, generally at night, in order to
guide him in his spiritual disciplines and to impart
Kabbalistic mysteries to him. It manifested itself in
the form of speech, which Karo recorded in his mystical diary. Some of this diary has been preserved as a
Kabbalistic homiletic commentary on the Torah.

Athanasius Kircher (1602–1680). Athanasius Kircher, Jesuit
and polymath, was born in 1602, in Geisa, a small
German town on the northern bank of the Rhone. His
father, Johann Kircher, taught theology to the monks
of the Benedictine house at Seligenstadt. Kircher
studied humanities at the Jesuit college in Fulda, and
in 1618 entered the Society of Jesus. He soon became
well-known for the versatility of his knowledge, and
in due course was celebrated as an accomplished
natural scientist and a great linguist, probing deeply
into the mysteries of ancient civilisations. In his lifetime, Kircher published over thirty books on virtually
every imaginable domain of knowledge. Following
in the footsteps of Marsilio Ficino and Pico della
Mirandola, he recognised that inspired truth existed

in nearly all religions of the past and with the assistance of his fellow Jesuits he accumulated a vast archive of reference material to support his investigations.[5] Through his work he became convinced that there had once existed a primordial tradition held in common by all humankind, and in his magnum opus, *Oedipus Aegyptiacus*, published between 1652 and 1654, he laid out his vision of the religions and beliefs of humankind emerging from one primordial stem—Egypt—which he considered to be the postdiluvian cradle of civilisation. In this remarkable book, which unfortunately has yet to be translated into English, Kircher gives an interesting account of the Kabbalah, including a particular arrangement of the Tree of Life that was subsequently adopted almost universally by European occultists. Indeed, the majority of non-Jewish expositions of Kabbalah, particularly those of a magical nature, have been influenced to some degree by Kircher. However, it should be noted that Jewish Kabbalists generally do not use his model.

Heinrich Khunrath (*ca.* 1560–1605). Heinrich Khunrath was born in Dresden or Leipzig, *circa* 1560. He received his doctorate at Basel in 1588, and practised medicine in both Hamburg and Dresden. He was a disciple of Paracelsus and a strong defender of the Doctrine of Signatures.[6] He defended twenty-eight theses on this subject to acquire his degree. He also worked tirelessly to develop natural magic from a Christian perspective; he sought to find the secret primary matter that would

---

[5] Most of which formed the basis of his museum of antiquities, curiosities and inventions located in the Collegio Romano.

[6] Doctrine of Signatures, a doctrine which maintains that all things in nature were divinely marked with a sign or signature that determined its purpose. In the mid 16th century this doctrine was applied in the field of medicine by Paracelsus. He developed a sophisticated table of correspondences based upon astrology. It was further popularised by Jacob Boehme in the early 17th century.

lead humankind into eternal wisdom. Although better known as an alchemist, Khunrath was also a proponent of Christian Kabbalah, which he believed to be the handmaid of true wisdom. This was reflected in his magnum opus, *Amphitheatrum Sapientiæ Æternæ* (published posthumously in 1609).[7]

Moses ben Shemtov de Leon (1240–1305). A Spanish Kabbalist, born in Leon, near Castile, Moses de Leon lived in Guadalajara and, from 1290, in Avila. He wrote some twenty Kabbalistic works but is best known for his revelation of the Zohar. According to Kabbalistic tradition, the authorship of the Zohar was attributed to the second-century Simeon ben Yohai. Legend has it that the Zohar was in the possession of the distinguished Kabbalist, Moses ben Nahmanides (1194–1270),[8] who sent it by ship to his son in Catalonia. However, the ship was driven off course by strong winds, and the manuscript subsequently came into the possession of Moses de Leon, who began transcribing and disseminating parts of it. Modern scholarship accepts that Moses de Leon was in fact the real author of the majority of the Zohar, but that later parts may be attributed to at least one other.

Isaac Luria (1534-1572). Isaac Luria was born in 1534 in Jerusalem. His father was a member of an Ashkenazi family from Germany or Poland, who emigrated to Jerusalem where he married into the Sephardi Frances family. When his father died, his mother took him to Egypt where he lived in the home of his wealthy uncle, Mordecai Frances. In Egypt, Luria

---

[7] The *Amphitheatrum*, now acknowledged as an alchemical classic, is an intriguing alliance of magic, Christianity, and Kabbalah; a combination that in 1625 brought upon it the condemnation of the Sorbonne. It has been republished many times, and remains popular to this day.

[8] Waite, *The Holy Kabbalah*, pp. 32–33.

studied under the Rabbis David ben Solomon Zimra
and Bezalel Ashkenazi. According to one account he
was introduced to the Kabbalah while in Jerusalem by
Kalonymus, a Polish Kabbalist. In 1569 Luria travelled
to Safed and began studying with Moses Cordovero.
Following Cordovero's death in 1570, Luria gathered
about himself a school of disciples, the most significant being Hayyim Vital. Central to Luria's teaching
is the doctrine of *Tiqqun* (restoration), which maintains that sparks of divine light have become trapped
within material things. Luria taught that these divine
sparks must be freed from their material servitude,
allowing them to return to their divine source. This
process is an interior, spiritual process whereby,
through acts of devotion in a meditative or contemplative state the divine sparks are raised up from their
fallen condition. On a personal level, Luria instructed
his students in meditation rituals whereby they could
emancipate themselves and achieve spiritual experience. He is recognised as one of the most influential
Kabbalists who ever lived, and regarded by many as
the preeminent Kabbalist of Safed. In his short life
he produced unique material that has been and is still
significant to practically all subsequent Jewish mystical creativity.

S.L.M. Mathers (1854–1918). Samuel Liddell MacGregor
Mathers was born in 1854 in the city of London.
In 1877 he was initiated into the Hengist Lodge
of Freemasons, where he became acquainted with
Frederick Holland, a student of Hebrew philosophy,
and probably through him became a member of the
Rosicrucian Society of England, thereby becoming
associated with doctors William Robert Woodman
and William Wynn Westcott—both who assisted

him with his studies. In 1887 he published a translation of Knorr von Rosenroth's *Kabbala Denudata*,
better known as *The Kabbalah Unveiled*. This book
earned him a considerable reputation and is still in
circulation today. Other works he translated were
The Sacred Magic of Abramelin the Mage and *The Key
of Solomon the King*. He also contributed various esoteric essays to the Rosicrucian Society's Transactions.
Mathers is probably best known for his role of co-
creator of the Hermetic Order of the Golden Dawn,
which was inaugurated in 1888. The impact this order
was to have on the world has earned both Westcott
and Mathers a place, albeit questionable, in the history of Kabbalah because the basic framework of the
Golden Dawn was Kabbalistic, and it opened the
doors for many people to engage with this obscure
subject. In 1890 he married Mina Bergson, herself a
member, and in 1891 he and his wife moved to Paris
where his fortune turned against him. He died during the influenza epidemic of 1918. He left a reputation for being a vain, conceited madman yet a gifted
magician with a real genius for magical ritual.

Giovanni Pico della Mirandola (1463–1494). One of the
most significant figures in the Italian Renaissance,
Pico della Mirandola was a very influential thinker
and scholar of his day. He was a member of the
Platonic Academy of Florence and a disciple of
Marsilio Ficino. He explored oriental studies when
it was not generally politically safe to do so, and was
a leading figure in introducing esoteric Judaism to
the Christian world, for which he became known as
the 'Father of Christian Kabbalah'. In 1486 he published *Conclusiones sive Theses* DCCCC, and invited
any who might wish to do so to come to Rome

and debate them in public; many of them were concerned with Kabbalah. According to Pico della Mirandola, the Kabbalistic approach to the scriptures demonstrated the truth of Christian religion. Unfortunately, some of his conclusions brought him into conflict with the church authorities, the debate never took place, and he was obliged to seek refuge in France.

Henry More (1614–1687). Henry More was born in Grantham, in 1614. In 1631 he entered Christ's College, Cambridge, where he was introduced to Neoplatonic thought. He was a spiritual genius and an important figure in British philosophy. Sir Isaac Newton knew him and was greatly influenced by him. Henry More represents the mystical side of the Cambridge Platonist movement; indeed, the Neoplatonic yeast that fermented within the school came to a head in his writings. He was in close contact with the preeminent Kabbalist of his generation, Knorr von Rosenroth, and in his *Conjectura Cabbalistica* (1653), More presented the essence of his philosophy in the form of an exposition of esoteric truths contained in the first book of Genesis. Subsequently he undertook a detailed study of the Jewish Kabbalah, being particularly influenced by Isaac Luria. Some of his studies were published in von Rosenroth's *Kabbala Denudata*. These studies sought to demonstrate that the Kabbalah contains, in a symbolic form, original truths of philosophy and religion, thereby exemplifying the compatibility of philosophy and faith.

Moses ben Nahmanides (1194-1270). Nahmanides was one of the most eminent members of the Gerona school. Also known as Rabbi Moses ben Nahman, or Ramban (Ramban being derived from his name Rabbi Moses ben Nahman), Nahmanides served as rabbi of Gerona. He was one of the leading authorities on the Talmud of his time, and was also recognised as a biblical scholar, poet, and philosopher. Some fifty of his written works have survived, most of which are concerned with the Talmud and Halakhah. In his later years he wrote a commentary on the Torah. At first, his intentions were to make this commentary a Kabbalistic commentary, but he changed his mind after he received in a dream a warning against such a venture. Consequently, there are many veiled references to Kabbalistic doctrine to be found in his commentary. Inevitably, throughout the thirteenth and fourteenth centuries, Kabbalists made considerable attempts to unravel its embedded secrets.

Israel Regardie (1907–1985). Israel Regardie was born Francis Israel Regudy in London, 1907, to poor Jewish immigrant parents. Regardie emigrated to the United States at the age of 14, and studied art in Washington and Philadelphia. He read widely and became interested in Theosophy, Hindu philosophy, and yoga. After reading material by Aleister Crowley, he initiated a correspondence that led to his returning in 1928 to the U.K. to become Crowley's secretary. The two men parted company four years later in 1932. In 1934, he joined the Stella Matutina, one of the branches of the Hermetic Order of the Golden Dawn. In due course Regardie acquired the bulk of the order's documents and published them in the infamous book, *The Golden Dawn*, a deed that earned him the enmity of the members and the reputation of being an oath-breaker for revealing some

of the core material of an order that was not only
still active but was to remain so until 1971. He published several books, the most significant being *The
Tree of Life*, and *A Garden of Pomegranates*. He died
in Sedona, Arizona, 1985.

Johann Reuchlin (1455–1522). Reuchlin was born in the
German town of Pforzheim, located in the Black
Forest. A humanist and Hebraist, he was one of
the foremost scholars of his day. He was ennobled
by Emperor Frederick III and served for more
than ten years as a member of the supreme court
of an association of German cities and principalities
known as the Swabian League. Reuchlin was also a
student of Pico della Mirandola. They met for the
first time in Florence in 1490. Convinced by Pico
della Mirandola that he should take the study of
Hebrew more seriously, Reuchlin studied with Jacob
Loans, the physician to Emperor Frederick III. In
1506 he published *De Rudimentis Hebraicis*, and in
due course published several other titles concerning
the application or use of the Hebrew language. His
passion for Kabbalah, a passion he shared with Pico
della Mirandola, was nourished by the conviction
that through Kabbalah we may recover the common
esoteric ground shared not only by Christianity and
Judaism, but by all religions. Following Pico della
Mirandola, he recognised in Kabbalah a profound
theosophical system that could be used in the rec-
onciliation of science and faith. His Kabbalistic
magnum opus was *De Arte Cabalistica*, published in
Haguenau 1517. The influence of the book is incal-
culable; it is without doubt one of the great classics
of its time, and what is more, it is now available in
English translation.

Knorr von Rosenroth (1636–1689). Knorr von Rosenroth, a Kabbalistic scholar and mystic, was born in 1636, the son of a Protestant minister in Silesia, at that time a region sandwiched between Austria and Poland, and now largely a part of Poland. While travelling throughout Europe with his father he came into contact with the mystical teachings of Jacob Boehme and was deeply affected by them. Later, while in Holland, he studied Kabbalah with some of the finest rabbinical minds of his day, being particularly influenced by the writings of Isaac Luria. He remained a student of Kabbalah throughout his life, and between 1677 and 1684 produced a two-volume summary of his studies, and a translation of some of the major Kabbalistic texts, titled *Kabbala Denudata*. This work was undoubtedly superior to anything that had previously been published by any non-Jewish source, and outside of Jewish circles was to remain the principal source of Kabbalistic ideas up until the turn of the twentieth century. In his own time he was reputed to have been the preeminent Christian scholar of Kabbalah and was in close contact with influential scholars and mystics such as the Cambridge philosopher Henry More and the Belgian mystic Francis Mercury Van Helmont (son of the last of the famous alchemists, Jean Baptiste van Helmont). Mathers's book *The Kabbalah Unveiled* is a translation of a part of the *Kabbala Denudata*.

Gershom Scholem (1897–1982). Gershom Scholem was born in Berlin in 1897. He was the youngest of four sons. Against his parents' wishes he started to learn Hebrew and attend the synagogue. In 1917 he left his parent's home and attended the University of Jena. He received his doctorate in Semitics from

the University of Munich, and his thesis—a translation and commentary of the Sepher ha-Bahir—was
published under the title *Das Buch Bahir*. In 1922
Scholem emigrated to Palestine and became the
head of the department of Hebrew and Judaica at
the National Library. His labours in the field of biblical research—particularly in the world of esoteric
Judaism—earned him the reputation of being one of
the foremost scholars of his generation. During his
life he traced, consolidated, and presented the historical background of esoteric Jewish mysticism that
is known as Kabbalah, and in doing so he drew it out
of the twilight zone of occultism and established it
as a true religious pulse that flows through the soul
of Judaism. His books on Kabbalah are invaluable to
any student seeking background information about
this subject. His major works include: *Major Trends
in Jewish Mysticism*; *The Origins of Kabbalah*; *On the
Kabbalah and Its Symbolism*; and *Jewish Gnosticism,
Merkabah Mysticism, and the Talmudic Tradition*. In
1968 he was made president of the Israel National
Academy of Science and Humanities. He died in
Jerusalem in 1982.

School of Safed. Safed is a town in upper Galilee, which
after the Jewish expulsion from Spain in 1492
became a centre of rabbinic and Kabbalistic activity. From 1530 onward Safed attracted rabbinic and
Kabbalistic scholars so that it became the focal point
for a Judaic spiritual renaissance. Thus from that time
up until about 1590 there evolved in Safed a distinctive Kabbalistic world view and religious way of life
that made Safed famous. It was formed in the main
through the influence of luminaries such as Joseph
Karo, Moses ben Jacob Cordovero, Isaac Luria, and

R. Hayyim Vital. In the sixteenth century Safed was
the centre of Jewish mysticism, indeed, the town was
numbered among the four sacred cities of the Holy
Land. It was also known as Beth-El, or the House
of God.

Sephardim. This word is said to be derived from the Hebrew
Sepharad (identified by some as Sardis, the capital of
Lydia), where a colony of exiles from Jerusalem was
established after the destruction of the first Temple.
However, from the beginning of the ninth century
Sepharad was also the Jewish term for the Iberian
peninsula[9] and throughout the Middle Ages the
term came increasingly to signify the descendants
of the Jews of Spain and Portugal. The Sephardim
spoke Judea-Spanish (Ladino). After their expulsion
from Spain in 1492, the Sephardim settled in many
parts of the world, including North Africa, Italy,
Egypt, Palestine, Syria, the Balkans, and other parts
of the Turkish Empire. Sephardic communities were
later established in western Europe, particularly in
Amsterdam, London, Hamburg, Bordeaux, and subsequently in the West Indies and North America.

Ezra ben Solomon (d. *circa* 1235). Ezra was one of the leading Kabbalists of his time and a key member of the
Gerona school. Little is known about him except that
he was often confused with Azriel. He wrote a commentary on the Sepher Yetzirah, and a commentary
on the Song of Songs that was printed under the
name of Nahmanides. He also wrote commentaries on the Talmudic legends. His writings show the
influence of his teacher Isaac the Blind, while he in
his turn greatly influenced both his contemporaries
and other Kabbalists throughout the thirteenth and
fourteenth centuries.

---

[9]   *Enyclopaedia Judaica*, vol. 14, p. 1164.

Hayyim Vital (1542-1620). Vital was born in Safed. In 1564 he began to study Kabbalah as a student of Moses Cordovero. When Isaac Luria arrived in Safed, Vital became his principal disciple, studying under him for two years until Luria's death in 1572. After Luria's death, Vital arranged Luria's teachings, putting them in written form. His notes on Lurianic Kabbalah were transcribed and published as *Etz Hayyim*. From 1590 he lived in Damascus, where he wrote *Sefer ha-Hezyonot* (Book of Visions), which contains records of his and other Kabbalists' dreams and mystical experiences. He also wrote many other Kabbalistic works and preached the coming of the Messiah.

Arthur Edward Waite (1857–1942). Arthur Edward Waite was born in Brooklyn, New York, on 2 October, 1857. His father was an American sea captain who died when Waite was very young. His mother was Emma Lovell, who when widowed returned to her home-land in England. Although his family was never well off and life was often a struggle, Waite was able to secure a basic education. When he left school he was employed as a clerk, writing verse in his spare time. Upon the death of his sister he became interested in spiritualism, and began to read regularly in the British Museum library, studying many branches of esotericism. In 1891, Waite joined the Hermetic Order of the Golden Dawn, and in 1902 became a member of the Societas Rosicruciana in Anglia. In 1915 he formed the Fellowship of the Rosy Cross, which embodied the mystical path rather than the magical. Waite was a prolific author, whose works were generally well-received in academic circles. He wrote on many subjects, including Rosicrucianism, Freemasonry, magic, Kabbalism, and alchemy;

he also translated several important mystical and alchemical works. A number of his volumes remain in print, *The Holy Kabbalah* being among them.

William Wynn Westcott (1848–1925). William Wynn Westcott, one of the foremost exponents of Hermeticism of his time, was born in the year 1848 at Leamington, Warwickshire. He was an esotericist, Kabbalist, ceremonial magician, and Freemason. He was active in the Societas Rosicruciana in Anglia (SRIA), before cofounding the Hermetic Order of the Golden Dawn with William Robert Woodman and Samuel Liddell MacGregor Mathers in 1888. He later became the Supreme Magus of the SRIA. In 1896, he abandoned his offices in the Golden Dawn because of a conflict of interest with his work as a Crown coroner, but he continued to head the SRIA and in his later years was involved with the Stella Matutina, a branch of the Golden Dawn. He is best known for his works *An Introduction to Kabbalah* and the *Collectanea Hermetica* series, both of which are still in print.

Simeon ben Yohai (fl. second century). Rabbi Simeon ben Yohai was a renowned *tanna* (a teacher of the Mishna),[10] in second century Palestine. He was one of five pupils of Akiba, who survived the doomed Bar Kochba revolt in the third decade of the second century. He was celebrated as a miracle worker and a master of hidden wisdom. His whole life was spent in devotion to the esoteric teachings that are now known as Kabbalah; indeed, for many centuries he was thought to be the author of the Sepher ha Zohar. Certainly Moses de Leon, who was the first to translate the Zohar, claims that he himself was not the author but merely the transcriber of the

---

10 Mishna: Commentaries and teachings concerning Jewish law, particularly those composed during the second and third centuries A.D.

original text. It is said that being accused of sedition, ben Yohai and his son Eleazar—fearing imminent death at the hands of the Romans—fled into the wilderness where they spent 12 years hidden in a cave.[11] There they spent their time in study and spiritual discipline, and were nourished by a miraculous spring and carob tree (some say date palm). It is thought that the secret wisdom acquired in their seclusion was embodied in the Zohar. Simeon frequently appears in the Zohar as a guide or teacher, not dissimilar, in my opinion, to Dante's Virgil.

---

[11] Both Waite and Myer give an account of this event in their books *The Holy Kabbalah* and *Qabbalah*, respectively. The account is taken from the Babylonian Talmud.

Appendix B

Glossary

Aaron. Elder brother of Moses. His name signifies 'the illuminated'.

Abba. Father. A symbol of Chokmah.

Abyss. The gulf that separates the three Supernals—Kether, Chokmah, and Binah—from the rest of the Tree of Life. The distinction is one of Unity and Duality.

Adam Kadmon. Primordial man

Adonai. Hebrew word for 'Lord' that is substituted for YHVH.

Agla. Notarikon for the Hebrew phrase, 'Thou art great forever my Lord'.

Amora. Name for the rabbis who were responsible for the part of the Talmud called Gemara.

Ancient of Days. A title of Kether, see Daniel 7:9.

Angel (Hebrew, *Malakh*). A supernatural being; a divine spirit that frequently acts as an intermediary between God and humanity.

Arikh Anpin. Long Countenance, a designation of Kether.

Assembly of Israel. A designation of the Shekhinah.

Assiah. The world of 'Making'.

Atbash. A code whereby the first letter of the alphabet is substituted for the last and so on.

Atziluth. The world of 'Emanation', the divine realm of Adam Kadmon.

Ayin. Nothing. Also a designation of Kether.

Beast of the Field. A designation for the higher angels.

Beehive. A symbol of the spiritual work concerned with the nature of industry and transformation.

Bereshith. In the beginning.

Beth Kol. A mystical voice of God heard from between the Cherubim.

Binah. Understanding. The third Sephira—the feminine principle—the great mother.

Boaz. The left-hand pillar that stood at entrance to King Solomon's Temple. The name *Boaz* means 'in strength'.

Briah. The world of 'Creation', of pure spirit and of archangels.

Chesed. Loving-kindness. The fourth Sephira, known as the Sephira of Mercy. Linked with the patriarch Abraham.

Chiah. In man it is the real life principle, the *vitalitas* as distinct from the more illusionary life of the physical body.

Chieftains. A term referring to the celestial guardians assigned to various nations on earth. According to the Zohar there are seventy such guardians.

Chokmah. Wisdom. The second Sephira, the masculine principle.

Daath. A point of conjunction of the forces of Chokmah and Binah. It signifies a point of gnosis; perhaps the highest point man can ascend to while incarnate.

Devekut. Clinging or cleaving. Applies to the union or communion with the divine.

Dibbuk. Possession by an evil spirit, or by disembodied souls seeking refuge in the body of another living person.

En-Sof. A Kabbalistic term for the hidden and unknowable God.

Enoch. The seventh pre-flood patriarch. He was the son of Jared and great grandfather of Noah. Such was his virtue that he was bodily taken into heaven, where he became Metatron, the greatest of all angels. The *Book of Enoch* is attributed to him.

Field of Apple Trees. Garden of Eden

Geburah. Strength. The fifth Sephira, known as the Sephira of judgement, also called 'severity' (*Din*).

Gedulah. A title of Chesed meaning 'greatness'.

Gehinnom. Hell, the place of eternal suffering for the wicked after death. Originally a valley southwest of Jerusalem where children were sacrificed to the gods Baal and Moloch.

Golem. A homunculus.

Gemara. Completion. A record of the sayings and discussions of the rabbis during the third to sixth centuries.

Gematria. A method of scriptural interpretation based upon the numerical equivalence of words.

Gilgul. Metempsychosis, 'reincarnation', or the transmigration of souls.

Guph. A body.

Haggadah. Homiletic exposition, legend or fable.

Halakhah. 'The Way'. Jewish laws.

Hashmal. Radiance.

Hasid. Pious. A member of a sect of pietists (Hasidim) that existed in Germany during the thirteenth century.

Hayyoth. 'Heavenly Beasts'; a class of fiery angels who support the Throne of Glory. They are the angels of Ezekiel'.

Hekhaloth. 'Palaces of Light'. A central feature of early Merkabah mysticism that refers to the seven halls or palaces through which the mystic must pass to gain entrance to the throne world.

Hod. Majesty. The eighth Sephira.

Husband. Chokmah.

Ishim. In Kabbalah the Ishim are the beautiful souls of just men and women; saints.

Jachin. One of the pillars that stand at the entrance of king Solomon's Temple, the other being Boaz. The name *Jachin* means 'establish'.

Kadmon. Primordial.

Kavanah. Concentration of attention in a spiritual discipline such as prayer or meditation.

Kavod. The divine glory.

Kedushah Sanctification. A prayer.

Kether. Crown. The first Sephira.

Klippoth. 'World of Shells' and demons and disorder.

Korban. Sacrifice, offering.

Lebanon (Cedars of). Six days of creation equating with the seven Sephiroth below the Supernals.

Lilith. The feminine power of evil.

Macroprosopus. The 'Vast Countenance' of God; a title of Kether, sometimes referred to as the 'long suffering'.

Malkuth. Kingdom. The tenth and last Sephira, the realm of the immanent Shekinah.

Melchizedek. Priest-king of Salem, an ancient name of Jerusalem; he is also known as the Prince of Peace, and the priest of the Most High God. His symbols are the chalice and a loaf of bread. In some legends he is also a personification of Enoch.

Menorah. A temple candelabra, usually with seven branches; often used as a symbol of the Tree of Life.

Merkabah. 'Chariot'. A vehicle by which the mystic ascends to, and enters into, the throne world.

Metatron. Angel of the Presence. He is believed to stand before the Throne of Glory and also guards the Halls of the Hekhaloth. He is also charged with the care of humankind. He is thought to be the angel who led the people of Israel through the wilderness.

Microprosopus. The 'Lesser Countenance' of God, consisting of the six Sephiroth Chesed, Geburah, Tiphereth, Netzach, Hod, and Yesod. Also referred to as 'The Short Face' or 'The Impatient'.

Midrash. A homiletical exposition of scripture.

Mishna. A collection of Jewish law, compiled in the early part of the third century.

Mitzvah. Commandment, particularly one of the 613 commandments of the Torah.

Mother letters. The three letters Aleph, Mem, and Shin, attributed to the three elements, air, water, and fire.

Nephesh. The lowest part of the soul, the instinctive or animal nature.

Neshamah. The highest part of the soul, the spiritual nature of man.

Netzach. 'Victory'. The seventh Sephira.

Notarikon. A system of shorthand where the letters of a word are seen as an abbreviation of a whole sentence, or conversely, where the initial letters of each word in a sentence form a word.

Pardes. Garden or orchard. An acronym for the four levels of interpretation of scripture, P = literal, R = allegoric, D = homiletic, and S = mystical.

Partsuf (plural: Partsufim). Countenance of God inherent in the Sephiroth. There are five main Parsuf that dwell in the realm of Atziluth. They are Arikh Anpin, Abba, Aima, Zair Anpin, and the Shekinah.

Patriarchs. The antediluvian progenitors of humankind from Adam to Noah, and in the postdiluvian era, Abraham, Isaac, Jacob, Aaron, Joseph, and David.

Pentagrammaton. A Greek word meaning 'five-lettered word' that refers to the Hebrew name *Yeheshuah.*

Pentateuch. The first five books of the Bible, attributed to Moses.

Prophet. A spokesman chosen by God to convey a message or teaching: 'If there be a prophet among you, then I, God, will make myself known to him—in a vision' (Num. 12:6). Prophets were frequently exemplars of holiness and devotion to God.

Rabbi. Teacher or master learned in Jewish law; evolved from the Pharisees in post-second Temple era.

Rasha. Wicked.

Ruach. The rational part of the soul.

Samael. Leader of the evil powers; his female counterpart is Lilith.

Sephira (plural: Sephiroth). Derived from the word for 'number'. The Kabbalistic term for the ten divine emanations or powers that constitute the revealed aspects of the divine.

Shekinah. The immanent divine presence. In Kabbalah the Shekinah is understood to be the feminine aspect of the divine, she is the Bride and is identified with Malkuth.

Shema. The fourth verse of Deut. 6, recited as a daily prayer.

Shemita. The sabbatical year.

Shofar. Ram's horn, sounded at the close of the Day of Atonement, and on New Year's Day.

Simple letters. The twelve letters that have one pronunciation, and which apply to the twelve signs of the zodiac.

Sitra Ahra. The other side, the power of evil.

Tallit. A fringed shawl worn by Jews when at prayer.

Talmud. The oral teachings of the Jewish people committed to writing between the second and fifth centuries, consisting of two parts: the Halakhah and the Haggadah.

Tannah. A teacher of the Mishnaic period—the first two centuries.

Targum. Aramaic translation of the Pentateuch.

Tephillin. Phylacteries consisting of two black boxes containing texts from the scriptures. They are tied during morning prayer, one to the left arm the other to the forehead.

Teshuvah. Repentance.

Temurah. A method of substituting letters according to specific rules. One of the most commonly known is *AiQ Bekar,* or the 'Kabbalah of Nine Chambers'.

Tetragrammaton. A Greek word meaning 'four-lettered word', invariably refers to the Hebrew name for God, YHVH.

Tikkun. Restoration, the restitution of order to the Sephirotic system.

Tikla. The scales that determine the condition of the soul.

Tiphereth. Beauty. The sixth Sephira; linked to Jacob.

Torah. Teaching. Specifically the Pentateuch, but also included the whole corpus of Jewish tradition.

Urim and Thummim. Parts of the breastplate of the high priest; they were used in the temple, before the Babylonian captivity, as a divine oracle. They have been defined as 'lights', 'gemstones', and 'perfections'. The true nature and appearance of them has been lost for more than two thousand years.

Wife. Binah.

Yehidah. The essential 'Self' the quintessence of the human personality, the highest state of consciousness.

Yeheshuah. A Hebrew form of the name Jesus; it is often called the Pentagrammaton and is associated with the four elements ennobled by the divine spirit of God.

Yesod. Foundation. The ninth Sephira.

Yetzirah. World of 'Formation', the world of angels.

Zaddik. Righteous.

Zair Anpin. 'Short Countenance'. The world of judgement, designating the Sephiroth from Chokmah to Malkuth.

Zizit. Fringes, particularly those on the tallit, or prayer shawl.

Zohar. Light, splendour, brilliance.

Appendix C

Suggested Reading

The following list of titles is designed to provide suggestions for background reading for the benefit of students of Kabbalah who wish to know more of its original setting, its development within the Western Hermetic Tradition, and of the symbolism employed. For your convenience, the most recent or accessible edition of all older titles is given, together with the original date of publication.

Blau, Joseph Leon. *The Christian Interpretation of the Cabala in the Renaissance*, Port Washington: Kennikat Press, 1965 (originally published in 1944).

Bond, F. B. and Lea, T. S. *Gematria, a preliminary investigation of the Cabala contained in the Coptic Gnostic books, and of a similar Gematria in the Greek text of the New Testament.* London: RILKO, 1977 (originally published in 1917).

Bosman, Leonard. *The Meaning and Philosophy of Numbers.* Berwick, ME: Ibis Press, 2005 (originally published in 1932).

Doresse, Jean. *The Secret Books of the Egyptian Gnostics.* London: Hollis & Carter, 1960.

Epstein, Rabbi Dr. I., trans. *The Babylonian Talmud*. London: Soncino Press, 1935.

Fortune, Dion. *The Mystical Qabalah*. London: Society of the Inner Light, 1998 (originally published in 1935).

Franck, Adolphe. *The Kabbalah: The Religious Philosophy of the Hebrews*. New York: University Books, 1967 (originally published in 1843; 1926 in English translation).

Ginzberg, Louis. *The Legends of the Jews*, 7 vols. Baltimore/London: Johns Hopkins University Press, 1998 (originally published in 1936-42).

Ginsburg, Christian D. *The Kabbalah: Its Doctrines, Development and Literature*. London: Routledge & Kegan Paul Ltd., 1956 (originally published in 1865).

Goldstein, David, trans. *The Wisdom of the Zohar*. Oxford: Oxford University Press, 1991.

Goodman, Martin and Sarah, trans. *Johann Reuchlin On the Art of the Kabbalah*. New York: Abaris Books, 1983.

Iamblichus. *On the Mysteries and Life of Pythagoras*. Thomas Taylor, trans. Frome: The Prometheus Trust, 1999 (originally published in 1822; 1818).

Kiener, Ronald C., trans. *The Early Kabbalah*. New York: Paulist Press, 1986.

Lenormant, F. *Chaldean Magic*. York, ME: Weiser, 1999. (originally published in 1877).

MacKenna, Stephen. *Plotinus: The Enneads*. London: Faber & Faber, 1962.

Mathers, S.L.M., trans. *The Kabbalah Unveiled*, London: Arkana, 1991 (originally published in 1887).

Menninger, Karl. *Number Words and Number Symbols*. New York: Dover, 1992.

Papus. *The Qabalah*. London: Thorsons Publishers, Ltd., 1977.

Philpot, Mrs. J. H., *The Sacred Tree*. New York: Dover, 2004 (originally published in 1897).

Regardie, Israel, The Tree of Life, St. Paul, MN, 1995 (originally published in 1932).

Robinson, J. M. *The Nag Hammadi Library in English*. New York: E. J. Brill, 1988.

Rolleston, Frances. *Mazzaroth*. York Beach, ME: Weiser, 2001 (originally published in 1865).

Rolt, C. E., trans. *Dionysius the Areopagite on the Divine Names and the Mystical Theology*. Berwick, ME: Ibis Press, 2004 (originally published in 1920).

Sperling, H., and Simon, Maurice. *The Zohar*. London: Soncino Press, 1931.

Stenring, Knut, trans. *The Book of Formation*. Berwick, ME: 2005 (originally published in 1923).

Stirling, William. *The Canon*. York Beach, ME: Weiser, 1999. (originally published in 1897).

Thompson, R. C. *Semitic Magic*, York Beach, ME: Weiser, 2000 (originally published in 1908).

Vermes, Geza. *The Complete Dead Sea Scrolls in English*. London: Allen Lane, The Penguin Press, 1997.

Waite, A. E. *The Brotherhood of the Rosy Cross*. New York: Barnes & Noble Books, 1993 (originally published in 1924).

———. *The Real History of the Rosicrucians*. Blauvelt, NY: Steiner Books, 1977 (originally published in 1887).

Williams, M. A. *Rethinking Gnosticism*. New Jersey: Princeton University Press, 1996.

Bibliography

Aquinas, Thomas. *Summa Theologia*. New York: Christian Classics, 1981.

Benko, Stephen. *Pagan Rome and the Early Christians*. London: Batsford, 1985.

Bible. The Holy Bible, New King James Version. London: Thomas Nelson, 1982)

Bible. The Septuagint version of the Old Testament: with an English translation and with various readings and critical notes. London: Bagster, 1879.

Budge, E. A. Wallis. *The Book of the Dead*. London: Routledge, Kegan Paul Ltd., 1969.

Charles, R. H. *Apocrypha and Pseudepigrapha of the Old Testament*. Oxford: Clarendon Press, 1913.

Cumont, Franz. *After Life in Roman Paganism*, New Haven: Yale University Press, 1922.

Cook, A. B. *Zeus, A Study in Ancient Religion*. Cambridge: University Press, 1914–1940.

Davidson, Gustav. *A Dictionary of Angels*. New York: Collier-Macmillan Ltd., 1967.

Dionysius the Areopagite. *On the Divine Names and The Mystical Theology*. C.E. Rolt, trans. Berwick, ME: Ibis Press, 2004.

Encyclopedia Judaica. Jerusalem: Keter Publishing House, 1971.

Feldman and Reinhold. *Jewish Life and Thought among the Greeks and Romans*, Edinburgh, T & T Clark, Ltd., 1996.

Folkard, Richard. *Plant Lore, Legends, and Lyrics*, London: Sampson Low, Marston & Co., 1892.

Iamblichus. *The Theology of Arithmetic: On the Mystical, Mathematical and Cosmological Symbolism of the First Ten Numbers*. Robin Waterfield, trans. Grand Rapids, MI: Phanes Press, 1988.

Josephus. *The Complete Works*. William Whiston, trans. Grand Rapids, MI: Kregel Publications, 1978.

Kaplan, Aryeh. *Meditation and the Bible*, York, ME, Weiser, 1988.

Kaplan, Aryeh, trans. *The Bahir Illumination*. York, ME: Weiser, 1979.

———. *Sefer Yetzirah*. York, ME: Weiser, 1990.

Khunrath, Heinrich. *Amphitheatrum Sapientiae Aeternae*. Hanover, 1609.

Levi, Eliphas. *Transcendental Magic, Its Doctrine and Ritual*, A. E. Waite, trans. London: Rider & Co., 1923. First published in French as *Dogme et Rituel de la Haute Magie* in Paris, 1856.

Myer, Isaac. *Qabbalah: The Philosophical Writings of Solomon Ben Yehudah Ibn Gebirol*. San Diego: Wizard's Bookshelf, 1988.

Pavitt, William and Kate. *The Book of Talismans*. London: Bracken Books, 1993. (Originally published in 1914).

Philo. *The Works of Philo*. C. D. Yonge, trans. Peabody, MA: Hendrickson, 1995.

Plato. *The Dialogues of Plato*. Benjamin Jowett, trans. Oxford: Clarendon Press, 1953.

Schenck, Kenneth. *A Brief Guide to Philo*, Kentucky: W.J.K. Press, 2005.

Scholem, Gershom. *Kabbalah*. Jerusalem: Keter Publishing, 1974.

———. *Major Trends in Jewish Mysticism*. New York: Schocken Books, 1946.

———. *On the Kabbalah and Its Symbolism*, London: Routledge & Keegan Paul, 1965.

———. *On The Mystical Shape of the Godhead*. New York: Schocken Books, 1991.

Shaw, Gregory. *Theurgy and the Soul*. Pennsylvania: Pennsylvania State University Press, 1995.

Tatlow, Ruth. *Bach and the Riddle of the Number Alphabet*. Cambridge University Press, 1991.

Thorndike, Lynn. *A History of Magic and Experimental Science*, 8 vols. New York: Macmillan, 1923-1958.

Waite, Arthur Edward. *The Holy Kabbalah*. New York: University Books, 1961.

Weistein, trans. *Gates of Light*. New York: Harper Collins, 1994.

Westcott, W. W. *Chaldean Oracles of Zoroaster*. In *Collectanea Hermetica*. York, ME: Weiser, 1998.

———. *The Kabbalah*. London: John Watkins, 1926.

———. *Sepher Yetzirah*, See Collectanea Hermetica. York ME, Weiser, 1998.

Index

About the Author

ALLAN ARMSTRONG, AN experienced Kabbalist, esoteric scholar, and skilled spiritual director entered the
Order of Dionysis and Paul in 1975, where he was introduced to the Kabbalah and its disciplines. In 1991 he became
Prior of the Order, which position he currently holds.